Women WORKING LOVINGLY *With* GOD

Dr. Patience E. Akinosho

© 2023 Dr. Patience E. Akinosho

All rights reserved. No part of this book may be used or reproduced by any means, graphic, electronic, or mechanical, including photocopying, recording, taping or by any information storage retrieval system without the written permission of the author except in the case of brief quotations embodied in critical articles and reviews.

Scriptures are taken from the KING JAMES VERSION (KJV), public domain.

Print ISBN: 979-8-35092-370-4
eBook ISBN: 979-8-35092-371-1

Printed in the United States of America

When you cry, you must see!
—Oluremilekun Ibitola Odeinde

You should never owe God. Rather, you should allow God to owe you.
— Abigail Agada Ejiogu

TABLE OF CONTENTS

AcknowleDgement	vii
Preface	1
Chapter 1: Introduction: Women and Their Assignments	4
Chapter 2: The Visitation by Archangel Gabriel: A Glorious Assignment	8
Chapter 3: Holy Mother Mary: Aligned with Glory	15
Chapter 4: Everlasting Eve: Evening of Life	26
Chapter 5: The Cooperative Praise of Rahab: Giving God Her Worse for God's Better	43
Chapter 6: Ruth And Hannah's Eyes: Winning God's Heart	59
Chapter 7: Anointed Esther: Guided by the God of Impossibilities	90
Chapter 8: The Shunammite Woman: A Serious Worshipper of God	104
Chapter 9: Conclusion: The Master Holy Spirit	127

ACKNOWLEDGEMENT

In loving kindness, I am immensely grateful to our loving Lord Jesus Christ! So sweet is He! We dedicate this book of women who are working lovingly with God, and all who love them, to God, the Father, God, the Son, and God, the Holy Ghost, who upended some existing thoughts and commissioned and hosted its writing.

I'm incredibly overwhelmed by the loving knowledge of our Master Holy Spirit in this book; His Hand of glory wrote the words you see here for our glorious learning.

Olusegun, my husband, your compassionate, caring, and loving heart is on full display in the way you help uplift, give hope, and bless society's vulnerable ones. Your gracious support of God's work and the selfless assistance you give to my efforts to help others fulfill God's purpose help enable the wonderful breakout of this book. You are lovingly committed and appreciated.

A foundational love of the grace for giving, in celebration of God's love for my growing family, is at the root of our gentle and gifted son. His heart for giving knows no end. We are grateful to

God Almighty who allowed him to heed his mother's cries for serious giving to help solve her many obligations, uplifting God's children, and celebrating our Father, God Almighty. We love you so, blessed by our honored God.

We give thanks to God for the wonderful insights provided by the soul of our growing family, our Mwanga (God's light), and our uniquely gifted and treasured daughter-in-law, Vanessa. Love, gladness, and joy of God to you, our princess.

A glorious resounding thanks to a woman of God, my auntie, the great Marion Yartey whose love, support, gracious praise, and worship uplifts and focuses my mind on tasks and keeps my mind on our loving and kind God, our Lord Jesus Christ. Special love to you, Auntie Me.

Glorious servant and honored of God, Sister Emma, your loving heart of support and joy of soul brings sunshine to an ordinary day. I bless the Lord, the Lifter of our heads, for your life and for the miracle of your eventual upliftment. I love how you take care of me, big sis, and how by our Master Holy Spirit's guidance, you stabilize rocky roads—treasured!

My very cooperative big sister, friend, and gatekeeper, Adanne Mercy Ebere, may God's blessings, multiple graces, and endless favor be upon you. Your blessed voice, loving support, counsel, and valued insights are joys to any ear in times of low energy, loneliness, and lack of laughter. I have loved you for them all!

I appreciate the man of God, Prophet Nana Bentil, for yielding to our Master Holy Spirit for instructions and inspiration. Your momentous spirit of guidance, the direction in the things of God's kingdom living, and the unusual winning spiritual strategies afforded you by our Master Holy Spirit have been of great help to many, including me, in this faith journey. Lovingly, we jointly appreciate our Master-directed winning insights from you, your giving heart, and your soft spirit. I join your congregation, the Master's Holy Mountain Embassy, in Gaithersburg, Maryland, to lovingly thank you for teaching and preaching straight from God's Word.

PREFACE

You are greatly beloved, Lord Jesus Christ. Our Master Holy Spirit asked me to write about women who are working lovingly with God to achieve purpose. I'm not sure why the assignment was given, but it might have had something to do with the work I was doing with a few young women at the time. These young women needed spiritual grounding in small doses and some immediate emotional help, all from a place of love. Truly, they were looking for the God who called us all to be carriers of His purpose, for they somehow felt lost and off balance.

We know the Bible is left for our teaching, reproving, learning, and mastery of God. But we may not always find that individual who can simplify God's Word for us without showing pride and judgment and who is devoid of personal prejudices.

Something wonderful happens when we gain the awareness that our righteousness is of God, through our Savior Jesus Christ. This helps us to understand that loving others, longsuffering, loneliness, and yielding to the Spirit of God are all part of our life journey.

We don't often have clear ideas or instructions about how to birth our divine purposes, and so we sometimes struggle through life. Our foundations do little at times to prepare us for the rigors of life. Our shield is God who enlightens, saves, and frees us from the many dangers.

Since this earth is not our home, we must be conscious of actions and words that impact our lives and prevent our making it to heaven and winning souls for our Lord Jesus Christ.

I was drawn to the story of the mother of our Lord Jesus Christ and the other women at the tomb of our Lord Jesus Christ. The eleven remaining disciples hadn't thought of sticking around and were afraid to anoint His body for burial. I was shocked to receive the revelation from our Master Holy Spirit that women were first to witness the resurrection of our Lord Jesus Christ because they are key to humanity's salvation and eternal life; we will see why.

God's assignment to Eve to return humankind to God was fulfilled by these women who knew their roles and who joyfully engaged with God over fear.

Our journeys to our own restoration may be painful ones, but women understand pain. God, in His awesomeness, built women with the capacity to navigate the twists and turns of mankind's restorative journey. We sin against God, but our loving Father has found powerful ways to restore us to our rightful place in His kingdom. He is God, our Lord Jesus Christ, Redeemer, King, and Savior.

I was made aware that women have a purpose on this earth to birth great things for God and mankind. Accordingly, with anything that happens to mankind, regardless of race and creed, women can help shape outcomes, bringing an air of greatness to them.

Holy Mother Mary, highly favored of God, when visited by Archangel Gabriel and given the momentous assignment to carry the Promised Seed, was very young. The task of leading mankind to their God, by way of Adam returning to eternity with God, was given to a young woman who graciously accepted her divine assignment.

We are not simply girls, women, and wives, but we are mighty instruments of great import in the hands of our Creator, Yahweh.

CHAPTER 1

Introduction: Women and Their Assignments

This book is about women working lovingly to impact humans' journey back to God, detailing also how God shows up in the affairs of humans. I excitedly paid special attention to the names and family backgrounds of our heroines, and you will see why.

God rested and began the work to reconcile people with Him, and the seven women that are the focus of this book contributed lovingly to that work. I have looked at them and their glorious assignments and roles, appreciative of their commitments and strengths.

Creation was over. Satan saw God removing a rib from Adam to make the woman Adam would later call Eve and moved to confuse Eve and take dominion over earth from Adam. But in the tapestry of her structure hid the looming Savior.

Generations later, a messenger angel visited Mary, and her name was changed to "blessed among women." From that moment, her womb transitioned in glorious expectation of the gift of our Savior. Our Lord Jesus Christ, God in man form—all God, all man—would come to take dominion of earth back from Satan, returning it to humans through the God-fulfilled work of these heroines and others not mentioned here.

In our complex loving nature, women are carriers of divine mysteries (servants of God, wombs). Victoriously, we are called to grow wombs to cancel the plantings of deceivers in our lives, families, and society.

Rahab (Joshua 2:1 KJV), a harlot whose house was a room in the wall of Jericho, saved the children of Israel. She gave Joshua's two spies information that helped him bring down Jericho's wall, which stood as a barrier to Israel getting to the Promised Land.

Only Rahab and her family were saved. This lowly daughter reminds us never to give up on our not-so-good children. She followed Israel to the Promised Land where she married Nahshon (whose name means "serpent") and gave birth to the victorious one, Salmon (whose name means "peace"), who lifted his generations and moved man closer to reconciliation with God.

Hannah, once barren and taunted by Peninnah, her husband's other wife, found the secret to God's heart in the posture of God's wonderful aging prophet Eli who was sitting by a post in the temple. She made a vow, honored her vow to God, and was surprised by the compassionate God. This mother of a prophet collided unexpectedly with an unauthorized woman, Ruth, both of whom moved mankind slowly to salvation.

Ruth, a Gentile, married Israel's Boaz as the result of a string of unpredictable but divinely coordinated events bringing humans back to God. Our Master Holy Spirit wonderfully shows us how Ruth (of Naomi) and Boaz (of Rahab) link us to the Garden of Eden, our Lord Jesus Christ, and the blessedness of loving others selflessly.

We can use the story of Queen Esther to teach today's young women looking for husbands about compassionate unseating of those now occupying their divine homes, grace in waiting, obedience to God's design for families, compromising self for the survival of others, and, last but not least, assuming an overtaker's posture to save generations to come.

Queen Esther was the woman who put everything on the line, risking her queenship to save her country. "And if I perish, I perish" (Esther 4:16). To help settle her during a period of unimaginable cruelty that was perpetuated against her people, the Jews, and even before she could become queen, God provided a protective covering for her. In the design of the palace garden, where she would reign, God hid divine messages and gifts to help her overcome.

The Shunammite woman's miracle child, a son, died suddenly on her lap. She gloriously positioned him in God's lap in the person of Prophet Elisha, for God alone has the power to override death and burial. Prophet Elisha was divinely placed, equipped, and armed by our Master Holy Spirit to go down to the Lord God and bring back the dead boy. Prophet Elisha's mysterious recovery of the boy from burial (grieving a life without God in it), a foreshadowing of God's power over death and burial, was a glorious display of God's power of love for His children.

We give all glory to our Lord Jesus Christ, our Master Holy Spirit, for the gracious women who went before us and laid the good examples we too hope to follow in our pursuit of God, offering our generation of women yet unborn the surprising wealth of joy.

Come with me and follow our Master Holy Spirit as He unpacks mysteries, offers solutions, builds stronger lives for His children, and raises us all to fulfill our purposes on earth.

CHAPTER 2

The Visitation by Archangel Gabriel: A Glorious Assignment

This book brings to life God's plans for mankind's salvation, showcasing the power of Holy Mother Mary as the carrier of the Promised Seed as well as other women winning their various assignments. The first of the seven women, Holy Mary, has a story that resonates with us all.

I wonder what the angelic visitation might have truly meant for young blessed Mary, highly favored of God. Her life would change forever. Her story tells us that events that may shake us to the core may momentously be our saving graces.

No growth in the spirit is ever easy. But when our loving God is involved in a situation, we can bet that His presence will have far-reaching rewards for all. Although He is all-powerful, God does not do things simply to demonstrate His power; He does them for the lifting of His children, to favor them, for the praise of His name and for revelation purposes, as in the redemptive purpose of our Savior's birth. The birth of our Lord Jesus Christ was prophesied by Prophet Isaiah (Isaiah 7:14) hundreds of years before it happened. Isaiah spoke of the Son of God who would be born unto us with the name Immanuel.

This is fulfilled in the Gospel of Luke 1 and 2 with the visitation of Angel Gabriel to a virgin named Mary who was espoused to the young man Joseph but selected by God for the divine assignment. Luke 1:28–32 lovingly reveals the birth of Jesus (though born of Mary, He was a child of the Holy Spirit) who would come to save the world, reconciling humans back to God. Our Lord Jesus Christ came to lovingly reveal to humans who God, the Father, is. He is an expressed image of the Father (Hebrews 1:3) yet was in our likeness to destroy the one who has the power of death (Hebrews 2:14–17).

Courageously, somehow victoriously, we know God and what He is like through His wonderful Son, our sovereign Lord Jesus Christ: holy, unusually compassionate, tenderhearted, forgiving to all who seek forgiveness, wonderfully gracious, and faithful is God. We know these things through Jesus Christ, our Lord, whose birth brought humans back to God.

Lord Jesus lovingly told Phillip, one of His disciples, before He ascended to be with the Father in heaven (John14), that He and the Father were one. Our Lord Jesus was part of God's redemptive plan, lovingly offering Himself as a substitutional sacrifice.

Our Holy Mary, who would birth our Lord Jesus Christ, found favor with God, and we can anticipate that changes ensued. Loneliness is rewarded by God! Mother Mary kindly leaned on

God for help, boldness, and guidance. She would be called blessed of God, the sacred birth would be in a lowly estate, the rest of the world would come to know her as the mother of our Lord Jesus Christ, and the glorious Son of God would reign as Lord, lovingly reconciling humans with God.

My own thought is that in many ways we women too would lovingly want to know how God can give up His own Son for others, for none of us could have borne what the special child Jesus would endure. We panic if our children suffer any minor illnesses, accidents, or harassment.

How can we bear to see our children trashed, abandoned, arrested, anxious, questioned, gaslighted, imprisoned, shamed, humiliated, crushed, beaten, disgraced, caused to fall under the unbearable weight of the wretched cross, nailed, killed, and buried?

Our Lord Jesus Christ experienced all the above, only to descend to Hades but rise again and ascend to the Father in heaven, to come again to live in believers as another comforter, our Master Holy Spirit!

Our Master Holy Spirit, in the writing of this book, told me that God came to save humans at a time when humans were searching fervently to know God. My own thought is that God came to lovingly answer the questions of the weary hearts who desperately were seeking to know Him for themselves. More than that, old doctrines about God were waning, and humans needed to know the one who created the heavens and the earth personally.

Apostle Paul, while in Athens, noticed the city had been given to idolatry and was heavily superstitious (Acts 17). Called to explain what the strange religion he was teaching meant, as Athenians spent much of their time in discussion of the latest new thing (religion), he called the people's attention to what he had found: their fervent worship "To The Unknown God" (Acts 17:23). Before then, the people either worshipped gods made by human hands, figments of their imaginations, or focused on the old doctrine of God. Apostle Paul reminded them that, by the birth of our Lord Jesus Christ, the Unknown God is made known to us.

From the time Holy Mary encountered the messenger angel, her womb transitioned in expectation of the gift of a Savior from God, and she was soon to be called Holy Mother Mary. Overlaying her assignment was the foreshadowing of enormous pain and uncertainty.

A change had entered Blessed Holy Mary's life; hers was a glorious position to be in. But the magnitude of the task would require she obey instructions she would not fully comprehend, and more than likely she would sacrifice herself, her loving family, and her privacy just to accomplish the loving assignment of birthing our Lord Jesus Christ.

Would you say yes to an assignment that would drastically alter your life? Can you imagine that, of all the women in the world, and through many generations, she was chosen for this glorious and awesome assignment? What in us would cause God to choose us for such a loving assignment? It may be easier for any one of us to accept this divine gift than it would be for us to commit to fulfilling it.

We are asked to grow spiritually. By listening to the angel sent from God, in that moment, Holy Mother Mary lovingly worked with God. All ungodly noises in her life were to be silenced (including fear and pride), for she had been lovingly moved in the spirit by our Master Holy Spirit, into a place of fuller understanding of God's purpose for mankind.

The holy words spoken by the angel of God ("And the angel said unto her, Fear not, Mary: for thou hast found favor with God. [31] And, behold, thou shalt conceive in thy womb, and bring forth a son, and shalt call his name Jesus." [Luke 1:30–31]) brought time into eternity and brought Adam (i.e., humanity) back to God, potentially to spend eternity with God. The benefits of our God and Blessed Holy Mary's cooperative ties are unfolding unendingly and will not stop doing so until the end of time.

Holy Mary agreed immediately to the responsibility of carrying the Promised Seed and made the trip to see her cousin Elizabeth. Her new role required that she connect with the one on earth who could understand the news she had just received, as her once barren cousin Elizabeth was carrying in her womb the forerunner of the Messiah, John the Baptist.

As the story unfolds, although not yet pregnant at the time of the divine pronouncement, Holy Mary's body, blessed among women, had to be prepared not only to hold a son, but also to host God's redemption plan. It was not just about a woman having a child— though birthing is among the best of the purposes for which her body was created—but also, through her pregnancy and the upcoming birth of our Savior, the salvation of mankind.

Who among us gives up the engagement to marry or honor for what seems like a not-so-solid plan? When God made the declaration that a Seed of a woman would bruise the head of the serpent, Holy Mother Mary wasn't there. Yet she simply accepted her divine assignment.

God did not hesitate to locate Mary in the spiritual season of change. Lord God knew that, from that time on, the earth on which she walked would bow to her as the fulfiller of a covenant made long before she was born. After all, the earth itself was present at the time God declared the decree to Satan about his impending head bruising, and now the earth too must do her part in protecting Holy Mother Mary.

The earth knew the fullness of the purpose of the soon-to-be blessed Seed in Mother Mary's womb and that "immortality" would not be corrupted in her (earth), even when the Promised Seed's time on earth is done and He is laid to rest in her (earth).

The earth obeys the voice of God. It meant she will be called upon to play a vital role of supporting, and not interfering with, the plans of God for humanity; the body of our Lord Jesus Christ would not see corruption (decay).

The earth has a mouth, stomach, eyes, voice, and ears. We know the earth heard the command of God, opened its mouth, and swallowed those who were contending with God's servant, Moses. (Numbers 16:32). That act was to demonstrate God's love for Moses and His power over the people, situations, and circumstances. Also, as recorded in Jeremiah 22:29–30, the earth was called to speak against the man Coniah, and he was declared barren (childless).

I was lovingly visiting family in Africa one summer. As I left the house to see other relatives around the village, I was told to be mindful of where I stepped, as my feet contain imprints of my destiny and anyone with access to the soil under my feet has the potential of negatively declaring evil over my life. To be sure no one would dictate the happenings in my life, I was told to collect the sand from under my feet and speak to it before venturing out. I then was encouraged to plead the blood of Jesus over it (and call on the blood of Jesus to speak, answer, argue, judge, arise, fight, and stand for me), in the name of Jesus. It was a display of their knowledge of the spiritual power of the earth on which we walk and how it can be used to change any life. I understood more clearly the positional privilege of belonging to our Lord Jesus Christ as I ventured out, for to Him wholly belongs the earth and all that is in it.

Our awesome God, our Lord Jesus Christ, should never be ignored in our lives and careers. When you know Him and the power of His saving graces, you are blessed beyond comprehension. You are conquering for others where they are lacking strength and bringing to the earth the fullness of God's love. His name, wherever it is voiced, changes situations and transcend all other powers.

Consciousness of our fears, and the limitations of our own power, makes us grateful for our loving relationship with our Lord Jesus Christ. The power of the Holy Spirit, our Master, even His fire, water, and wind, given to us by our Lord Jesus Christ, remains available still for our use in the battle of life. We too must be willing to do the will of God, regardless of the assignment.

The earth knew just what to do to the wounded Christ. It protected blessed Holy Mary and the Promised Seed, and our crucified Lord Jesus Christ did not face corruption in burial but rose again on the third day.

CHAPTER 3

Holy Mother Mary: Aligned with Glory

Let us continue to examine a very special topic given by our Master Holy Spirit. We are easily bruised but not broken, crushed not buried. We are who we are made to be, in the likeness of God.

We continue with Holy Mother Mary to examine how this special young woman lovingly worked with God. First let's note these important points about her:

- God chose her to bear the Promised Seed, our Lord Christ Jesus.
- She rejoiced, was blessed among women, and was highly favored.
- She was blessed, would be holy, and was visited by Archangel Gabriel who stands before God.
- Holy Mother Mary wondered why she was stopped by the angel but did not hesitate to listen to his divine message.

- Good tidings were poured on her by the angel.
- Holy Mother Mary made a polite visit to her pregnant cousin Elizabeth, carrier also of a Divine miracle.
- The winning child in Elizabeth's womb leaped for joy upon hearing Mary's voice.
- Elizabeth confirms her cousin Mary as the Holy Mother of her Lord by her speakings.
- Lovingly, Holy Mother Mary accepted her life-changing assignment.
- Our Lord Jesus Christ, in truth, fulfilled His loving reconciliation assignment.

The birth of our Lord Jesus Christ was the first part of her assignment. When the child Jesus was presented to God in the temple on the eighth day, God's special man Simeon was there, for God had promised he would not die before seeing this special child, the coming Messiah. His observations increased this mother's awareness of her Son's impending death. The wicked would be given winning graces to crucify her innocent Son.

Our Lord Jesus Christ was 100 percent God and 100 percent human. He would suffer greatly for all mankind but would teach the truth about the love of God; set free all that are held captive; teach about obedience to God; heal the sick; cleanse the leper; raise the dead; cause the lame to walk; feed the hungry; open the eyes of the blind; elevate disgraced and forgotten women; be crucified, die, and be buried; restore humans; bring humans back to their God; help humanity love itself; and sit at the right hand of God. Her gloriously gracious spirit for service would lovingly be built by God.

In offering up herself, Holy Mother Mary joined God in His victorious loving of humans. At the wedding at Cana of Galilee, Holy Mother Mary was the one who, knowing her role in our Lord Jesus Christ's loving earthly ministry, called on him to supernaturally make wine available to the gathering of thirsty guests. We plan to examine this further in this section.

The God of her forefather Abraham, whom she trusted, would protect her, preserve her, and make her strong by His Spirit. We too, if invited to an event or place, must ask God how our gifts and talents can be used at that place, in the moment.

One day, I received in my spirit the need to return a blouse I had bought for a friend. I was visiting my friend at the time. It was a bit small and was not her color. I kept it for a few days, wondering whether I should give it to someone else. But on this fateful day, I had the urge to return the blouse to the store. Upon getting there, I decided to buy a small hand towel for the bathroom as well. I picked up what I needed, hoping to pay, find a new blouse, and then leave the store. I picked up the hand towel and proceeded to look for the blouse. Hindsight being 20/20, I now know that none of what was happening with me in the store was of my own doing.

I walked toward the blouse racks, and the little towel I was holding fell to the ground. I knew our Master Holy Spirit was speaking, letting me know not to take the towel home. I was going to just leave the hand towel on the clothing table in front of me when our Master urged me to take it back to the towel section. He asked that I turn on the audio Bible app on my phone to Psalm 3, listening as I walked back. I did just that, being mindful of the volume as I did not want to impose on other shoppers. I was motioned forcefully, my body now being under the control of our Master Holy Spirit, to go to the back of the aisle with my phone on Psalm 3. I complied. Upon getting there, I realized two adolescents were on the floor making out—sweeping the floor with their bodies, so to speak. Other shoppers were passing, and none stopped to say a word of decency to the unusual lost teens.

I upped the volume on my phone. They could not bear the anointing from the Word of God coming loudly from me standing next to them. I was no longer afraid of other shoppers. Our Father was trying to avert a disaster. Other shoppers seemed disinterested in two undisciplined (controlled by the Old Serpent) teens making out in public view.

There's power in the Word of God. But the Old Serpent looking to battle with our Master Holy Spirit had these teens' wildness at full blast in public. I stayed next to them and would not budge; nor would I lower the volume. Our God needed me to step up, so I lowered the fear in me. The Old Serpent could no longer bear hearing the fiery words. Suddenly they could not bear hearing the sacred Word of God any longer either, and they ran out of the store. Job accomplished, I proceeded to search for the blouse.

The Lord then urged me to switch the Bible app to Psalm 6 and go to the aisle I had in mind. I have learned to follow the movement of my body in such situations, and He was again in control of my body.

I turned the volume up just enough for it to be heard. I got nearer to the aisle of interest. There a young woman was looking through the racks. She was drawn to me—well, to Psalm 6—and proceeded to whisper something to me. She asked whether I liked reading the psalms, and I smiled and gave her a nudge. It wasn't what I was expecting. I had expected her to say it was too loud for her hearing, something I was already afraid would happen.

The young woman stretched her head across the clothing rack and whispered to me, "Can you help me? I see things. I see them ever y night, and I can't sleep." She then asked for the psalm I had playing on my phone. I was concerned as to what the Lord wanted. She asked for my number. I hesitated, and then she asked for my email. I gave that to her. I hung around for a moment and realized she was partly the reason why I was there. I hurriedly picked out a new blouse, made the exchange, and left.

I was overwhelmed with what had happened that day, but I then began questioning myself about whether they had happened at all. I called my spiritual father, Prophet Nana Bentil, and shared the experience with him. He was the only one I believed could understand what had happened. The fear of losing my mind was real. He assured me that it had happened and began praising our Master Holy Spirit. He also prayed our faithful Father would protect me, because I had been in a battle for souls for the Father, our Lord Jesus Christ.

Still, I was a bit nervous. I waited for a few days for the young woman to send an email to confirm the incident had taken place, for the Old Serpent had convinced me it had not. The young woman's email came a few days later, not a moment too soon. I ran to share the story with my friend Emma, the one I was visiting at the time. Prior to that, I had been scared to say anything.

We prayed together, and I allowed her to share her fears, vague belief in God, and her experiences. She did so over several days, each time becoming a little less fearful and stronger in the Lord. We remain friends. Our Lord Jesus Christ had set her free, and whom the Son sets free is free indeed. She is now a strong, victorious foot soldier for our Lord Jesus Christ.

Our Lord Jesus Christ turning water into wine that night was the foreshadowing of the divine connection of humanity to the old table of shewbread, the upcoming glorious feast of bread (His body) and wine (His blood) at the last supper.

Most favored among women, Holy Mother Mary found her eyes (vision) and ears (obedience) guided and directed by the God of her life. Just as the Spirit of God lovingly hovered over the waters of the deep in the beginning of creation, as darkness covered the deep, He was covering the six stone water jars outside the ceremonial hall, each of which held the twenty or thirty gallons of water our Lord Jesus Christ had asked for. It was these six (humanity) jars of water (our Lord Jesus Christ) that were turned to wine (branches in the Vine), introducing us to our Lord Jesus's ministry of mankind's salvation, gaining wholly our freedom from Old Serpent's domination. His beloved mother had asked for that favor. Did we ever stop to think why that miracle occurred?

The Master Holy Spirit is teaching us that we can overcome impossible situations by relying on God. It wasn't an arbitrary decision on the part of our Lord Jesus Christ. Follow me as our Master Holy Spirit opens this seemingly vague miracle of our Lord Christ.

Jesus somehow turning water into wine, connecting us to the Garden of Eden where Adam and Eve lived a reality that God had created for them but failed to sustain . . . He showed up in the

Garden of Eden as the Old Serpent to alter Adam and Eve's reality that God had with them. Wine can alter a person's reality.

Eve didn't seem dead after eating of the fruit, so Adam thought. But the separation from God would conclude, as Adam would eat of the fruit in the garden God had asked them not to eat. Sinning wouldn't end there, as other sins would follow suit. Their first son, Cain, killed his younger brother, Abel, bringing to life other sins that we have now normalized: unbelief, greed, reopening of old hurt, deception, lying, fear, hatred, bitterness, disobedience, betrayal, weariness of soul, backbiting, jealousy, stealing, idolatry, and many more.

Some people see wine as uplifting for their spirit—a distorted reality, of course. Drinking alcohol at the very least can impair rational thinking, cause illnesses, destroy families, wreck destines, and give breath odor. One can very easily move into the Old Serpent's turf in an impaired state.

Thus, the miracle of wine gives increased insight into our Lord Jesus's plan for humans' victory over the Old Serpent. We are reminded that we are cocreators with God as transformed beings. Our Lord Jesus Christ came from heaven to earth to change humans' reality, transform humans, and bring humans (Adam) again to God.

Remember that our Lord Jesus Christ was ushered into His covenant ministry by His Blessed Mother. She was the carrier of the covenant that would destroy the works of Satan over lovers of God. The beloved Son of God was carried in Holy Mother Mary's womb, the ground of planting. As with any other pregnant mother, He had communicated with her some divine truths, as He was being nurtured in the secret place of her divinely commissioned womb, the soil of His glorious covering. She kept these mysteries secret in God, for He honored her sorrow, and we too would come to know them and fear God.

In obedience, Holy Mother Mary and His good earthly father Joseph managed their privileged grooming of the beloved Son of God, keeping secret any information they had of His divinity until He was ushered into ministry at the rightful age of thirty, living only as a boy, doing His chore as the son of His earthly father, before the ministry of salvation was born.

Before then, only at age twelve did we see and hear Him at the temple, "sitting in the midst of the doctors, both hearing them, and asking them questions" (Luke 2:46). Our Lord Jesus Christ was showcasing His divine authority over the Word, for He is the living Word. Here the source of sorrow that would plague His ministry was laid bare; these temple experts would orchestrate his crucifixion as a 100 percent man. It was He who willingly, not by their force, gave up His life for mankind. By His crucifixion on the cross of Calvary, His blood, poured out for us, stands as a powerful weapon against the works of the devil.

We know that, early in the ministry of our Lord Jesus Christ, the miracle of wine (changing water into wine) was to draw our attention to the distorted image of humans. Wine, gloriously from our Lord Jesus Christ, brings us graciously to His realm of possibilities and answered prayers, giving honor to the one who created all things.

Our Lord Jesus Christ taught His disciples to pray as in Matthew 6:10 that His will be done on earth as in heaven. Those who choose to lovingly surrender to the will of our Lord Jesus Christ for righteous living here on earth are united in minds, thoughts, and deeds with Him. His perfect holy "will" lovingly leads us to a place of abundance of life (light, love of God, blessings, love of others, joys, giving to others, riches, and more).

When our Lord Jesus Christ changed water into wine, He was taking us back to our origin—the holiness of God who was present in the Garden of Eden with Adam and from whom he had moved away. But this new wine, the blood of Jesus—not the old wine that gave a distorted view of God, instigated by the Old Serpent—brings us to a place of blessings from God.

More than anything, wine collection is a process that elevates aging to a new level, though it may eventually oxidize and lose its drinkability. A one-hundred-year-old wine surpasses a one-day-old wine in quality and taste, though it may not be drinkable after a point. This lets us know that the perfect wine for believers is the blood of Jesus. By extension, the old defeat across time and space—as though it happened only yesterday—reversed by the crucifixion and resurrection of our Lord Jesus Christ, wins new victories for mankind.

Holy Mother Mary ushering our Lord Jesus Christ into ministry means that we too must elevate the role of women in our families, workplaces, churches, communities, schools, courts, and society to fully reign on earth.

Praying mothers need the support of their spouses in growing children for our Lord Jesus Christ. We must uphold our relationship with Him. We must not be given conditions by which we must pray in our homes; dinner can wait.

Many mothers are badgered or neglected in their homes. Many still are goaded by their spouses for being gifted to pray for mankind.

So husbands consider them boring or unsexy for being consumers of scriptures, God's holy words. Much of our battles are not physical, for they are not with flesh and blood but with principalities and powers and forces of wickedness in high places (Ephesians 6:12). This means many of our victories achieved through prayers also may not be seen in the physical world; but women, we must keep praying.

Like Holy Mother Mary, our praying mothers bring the presence of God into time, and our homes are better for it, whether we notice Him or not. The Bible tells us to pray without ceasing. Without doing so, our homes are opened to the interferences of the Old Serpent, vain glorification of earthly things. Children, and society at large, may pay the price of our homes without God in them, as God is love and loving Him helps us more easily love one another.

Daughters of God ask and receive blessings for maintaining their homes. They ask also and lovingly receive common blessings and graces for maintaining who they are: bold deliverers of the weak to God, great light givers, burden bearers, divine connectors and location aviators, ministers of the gospel of peace, lonely solution carriers, facilitators of liaisons, and givers of self to mankind.

We are aware that blessings of God are always accompanied by major complications of life and other local challenges. We are more than equipped to overcome them.

Women help deliver mankind from destruction. Holy Mother Mary courageously carried the Promised Seed that brought us believers the better covenant of the blood of Jesus, a sacrifice of self for mankind. Women, we are friends of God. We rise in the order of our Holy Mother Mary to birth, usher all into the newness of our Lord Jesus Christ, and help God's children fulfill their purposes in life.

Yet we are not to use our corrected reality, our resiliency, and the power of knowledge to bring down the very ones we were meant to help save: our spouses, our children, relatives, parents, friends, and colleagues. When we don't have control over our words and actions, we position ourselves as adversaries of God.

CHAPTER 4

Everlasting Eve: Evening of Life

We give glory to our Lord Jesus Christ for His mercy and grace, which enabled four of His loving daughters to move strategically to help one of His strapped ones. The underpinning of sexual curiosity had lovingly overwhelmed her soul. God, in His holy Word, lets us know that where there is a lack of information awareness and understanding, people do perish.

Enemies of God had targeted one quarrelsome girl for destruction, attempting to derail her destiny. Without knowing it, she was causing confusion at home, calling down the Old Serpent to oversee the affairs of the family.

Though she was blessed with gratitude, love, and a grateful heart for our Lord Jesus Christ, around this lowly anointed daughter of God were manipulators beholden to the devil, willing to corrupt loving young girls. Cunningly, she left her loving home for the street in the similitude of leaving the presence of God.

Greatness, love, and the light of our Lord Jesus Christ were in this daughter. Lord Jesus has left us the graces and blessings for the deliverance of His lost children. This loving soul retriever lovingly brings back other young girls experiencing grass withering (giving life where the lack of joy had once found a home) to the loving comfort of self-love and blessed covering of God.

Many young girls in this situation, where sexually consuming fire is winning, find the wickedness of suicide, low self-esteem, running away from home, and mining in fire soil (the old mine of Satan, giving up their virginity to predators) to be preferred options.

Four great women with various God-given gifts (loving gifts of heart healing, praise, deliverance, and blessing of money), gathered to

- provide victory by the victorious power of God's right hand of righteousness,
- use baked bricks (financial resources) to honor the winning girl,
- ensure victory over the Old Serpent's lies of not being good enough,
- show her she was more than a conqueror and that she was fearfully and wonderfully made,
- lead her to our Lord Jesus Christ, our Master Holy Spirit, for mercy and self-forgiveness, and
- provide answers on how to fight enemies of progress released against her.

We know that had this young girl been left alone in her wandering off, the no-good, lying Satan could have messed up the evening of her life, potentially aborting her destiny. We each have passed this way before, each of us experiencing a degree of what God's daughter experienced.

Our Lord Jesus has made us servants to His knowledge of knowing, seeing, hearing, and reacting. Our God had sounded a great deliverance call for action. By His grace, we had all gathered to uphold the covenant of loving and supporting one another, for we are all His own. Otherwise, God's chosen one would have experienced an unholy fall from grace.

Guided by the Finger of God (our Master Holy Spirit), as the lines had fallen for her in pleasant places, this chosen one is now living comfortably with family and fulfilled in Christ Jesus. Hallelujah!

It appears that the subject of Eve should have been the first one we tackled. But our Master Holy Spirit did not give the text to me in that order. He asked me to place this topic here for reasons unknown to me. It seems fitting that, after introducing Holy Mother Mary, we can go back and see her ancestor, so to speak, the one from whom she earned the right to bear the holy Promised Seed and from whom, by grace alone, believers would receive forgiveness.

I had just finished my devotional time with our God, Lord Jesus Christ, and was looking forward to receiving instructions for the day ahead—a grace only He can give mankind. The first instruction I received was to go back and continue to work on this book. I may never know how important this book is both to our Lord Jesus Christ and to His delicate children who will come to read it.

By the Spirit of God, our Master Holy Spirit, I had selected seven women in the Bible whose lives He wanted to examine for our benefit. He added Blessed Mother Eve, and my first thought was, "I see that it makes sense, so I will put her first, not Holy Mother Mary." But I was told to reverse the order. So here we are!

The Master Holy Spirit, be pleased that she is placed here, and I ask all to go along with me to see what He will reveal about her to us all. We might receive a new insight to help us in our walks of faith and in our world today.

I write not of my own skills, but as our Master Holy Spirit helps, guides, directs, and leads. Our Lord Jesus Christ, when He was on earth, told His disciples that the Son does nothing on His will but His Father's will (John 5:19).

We all ought to follow Jesus Christ as a model of obedience if He gives us the grace of service to God. Our Master Holy Spirit was lovingly given to us by our Lord Jesus Christ, after His resurrection, before He ascended into heaven, to guide us in our honoring of our Lord Jesus Christ, among other things. Our Master Holy Spirit has given me a few revelations to add to our body of knowledge of the kingdom, in this dispensation. Any light we receive for our generation, and for those yet unborn, will bless us all.

As I pondered on what to write about Eve, I was reminded that God took a rib out of Adam to form her. I am reminded too that Adam was put to sleep as that was going on, giving us the first surgery ever done. It seems God was also laying the groundwork for both our scientific and our medical knowledge.

We must not assume that Adam's sleep was like what we experience today where we go straight to dreamland for a few hours, whether we remember our dreams or not. I profess that what occurred with Adam was different and unique, for creation was still in progress and everything was still taking shape, including the newness of sleep.

I profess that to be asleep is to allow the body to relax for a few hours. But God had not rested at this point of creation. Adam was still a spirit being, one who saw God in the garden and communed with Him daily. Bear in mind that Eve was still inside of Adam, for God said He made them male and female, and she was yet to be separated from him (Genesis 1:27; 2:21).

We take the posture of the fruit of the righteous kind, worthy and pleasing to God. Adam was now part of the garden, having been created last, and had everything handed over to him by God. And in him was Eve, in the similitude of a seed in a yet-to-bloom fruit tree. Trees in the Garden of Eden had seeds in them. A tree with seeds—Eve—was still inside Adam.

When God loves us, there's nothing He will not do to ensure our needs are met. He sees our needs before they become evident to us. God noticed Adam alone, although surrounded by all the animals. God knew His lowly Adam, alone or depressed, given our current knowledge of humans, needed a companion. God, our Maker, surgically took a rib from Adam (man) to form the woman. When Adam opened his eyes to behold the beauty that was "the light in the tunnel," Eve, the only thing he could say was, "Woman."

A man of God, Nana Bentil, reminded me that as a spirit man, carrier of the breath of the Almighty, it goes without saying that

Adam was monitoring everything that God was doing during the making of Eve, though he was himself asleep in God.

Prophet Nana Bentil, a very anointed man of God, and my father in the Lord, pointed out that Adam called out "woman" because he had already seen her form in the spirit. She was no stranger to him, so when awoken from his sleep, he couldn't say to God, "Who is this?" Rather, when he awoke from his sweet sleep of glorious change in atmosphere, his excitement was reflected by him saying, "Woman!" (cocreator.)

Our Master Holy Spirit gave me an insight on what He says the word "woman" means. Adam (the earthly man) called the female (resolute man, with womb) who was taken out of him "woman." The online Oxford Languages defines "female" as "of or denoting the sex that can bear offspring or produce eggs, distinguished biologically by the production of gametes (ova) that can be fertilized by male gametes" (https://languages.oup.com/google-dictionary-en/).

However, by divine instruction, let's break down the word "female" further.

Fem = no more atmosphere of aloneness, separate but alone for a moment

ale = great in the one (Adam), is his other

We are made aware that a power in Adam would help him, leading him to dominate the earth God had given him to tend. Daughters of God, lions, do you see how much of a threat you are to the kingdom of darkness?

When Adam was alone, he was of no threat to Satan who had been thrown down to earth from heaven. As soon as the woman arrived on the scene, Satan, now the Old Serpent, had to devise a plan to abort her assignment to help lowly Adam dominate earth.

In the tapestry of Eve, the woman, was the mystery of the salvation of mankind. Adam blurted out "woman" because she was the bone of his bone, as our Master Holy Spirit shared, but this also lets us know that everything about her was carved in who she was. Hidden in Eve's structure was the capacity to bring forth goodness—wonderful, our Lord Jesus Christ.

Our Master Holy Spirit pointed out to me that inherent in the word "woman" (an adult female [https://languages.oup.com/google-dictionary-en/]) is an attribute of our Lord Jesus Christ: wisdom. Our Master Holy Spirit loosely broke down the word "woman" to me this way, noting the Seed in the woman will possess the wisdom to overcome man's adversary:

Wo = The man (Jesus) of the male (Adam) was in the woman (Eve) in his ribs.

Man = Earned evening (problem) in earth (Adam and Eve) will birth Him (Jesus).

The decision by God to rescue humans from the fall was also inherent in the living beauty (the woman) who had power to subdue Satan who had been a presence in the garden. Thus, the coming of our Lord Jesus Christ was ordained and hidden in the man (Adam) even before the fall.

God made the earth for humans. But Satan, once a worshipper of God, an anointed Cherub, had been defeated and thrown out of heaven and had fallen into the deep (water from the Spirit of God). He was now trying to lay claim over the earth God had made for humans, but God called forth light to subvert his actions in the deep and began the process of creation. Earth will be uplifted from the deep (authorized water from heaven). Adam was made from the earth (with water from the deep in it), uplifted, and given dominion over it.

Then Satan devised a diabolical plan to take it from him. When he tricked the woman, causing Adam to disobey God, Satan succeeded in taking dominion over the earth from Adam. He saw Eve as the very vile creature that came to take his possession from him. The two were now driven out of the glorious presence of God and into that of God's enemy, Satan. As they left the garden, Adam named his wife, the bone of his bone and flesh of his flesh, Eve.

Eve (Chavah/Havah, chavah) "(to breathe, and chayah, to live, or to give life); the traditional meaning of Eve is life or 'living'. It can also mean full of life, and mother of life" (HYPERLINK "https://en.wikipedia.org" https://en.wikipedia.org).

Part of the meaning of her name, Eve, among other meanings that have been shared with those who have received insight from our Master Holy Spirit, and other insights yet to be shared, denotes one who would have communion with God and is given dominion to multiply but who sins and will give birth to a generation that will birth one who will die but will rise again from death and will be given the power to overcome Satan.

Let's look at the breakdown of her name, as our Master Holy Spirit shared with me, more closely.

E = In the loving breath of God (the glory of God has departed from us, evening has come).

ve = made from unstable earth, and all of him now out of him; Adam received a major reason to lose the covering of God (light).

Our man, Adam, was saying the loving-kindness of God displayed in God's glorious love for humans gave him the ability to choose, and selecting to choose unwisely, he had fallen.

The Master Holy Spirit was letting us know that, though of earth, man in the likeliness of God was made possessing God's momentous love, glory, honor, rest, and goodness. God always appealed to the spirit in man, but Satan appealed to man's unstable nature (flesh). Yet the same one that fell for his lies will be used to defeat him and win back mankind's glory.

Adam named his wife Eve. It was a demonstration of the true humility that our Lord Jesus Christ who came as a descendent of Eve and whose Heels (i.e., His Word and the eventual salvation of God's people, among other mysteries known to God) will bruise the head of the serpent.

The scriptures tell us that, to create the woman, God put Adam to sleep and then took a rib from his side. God wanted to show what would happen to mankind when the Savior comes to save them.

Soldiers who were at our Lord Jesus Christ's crucifixion pierced His side (womb in the spirit). He still hung on the cross when He was pierced. They needed to confirm He was dead and could be buried before Sabbath. He was. Still, when they pierced Him, water and blood came out of His righteous side. He, repeating the surgery done on Adam to birth Eve, brought to full circle words spoken in the Garden of Eden to Eve, Adam, and the Old Serpent, for Satan was once again present at the crucifixion of the second Adam (our Lord Jesus Christ).

Our Eve has been a compelling subject for us to discuss. She reminds us that at creation, even when children are still in the wombs of their mothers, they are given assigned roles and purposes to fulfill for God and for mankind.

The woman, Eve, failed in her purpose in time and space, compromising her destiny, but her children will be saved by the substitutional offering who came out of her generations, Mother Mary's womb, our Lord Jesus Christ, to reconcile humans to God.

There are a few notable things about our Mother Eve that every woman working lovingly with God needs to know:

- the importance of follow up
- not to be socially susceptible to idleness
- not to divulge information she ought to keep
- to be mindful of the spirit of lust

The story of Adam and Eve, their creation story, shows us that Eve walked away from her responsibilities, leaving her, in the similitude of David, vulnerable to deception.

Adam was assigned to dress and keep the garden (Genesis 2:15). Eve left Adam to tend the garden alone, wandering off. In choosing to take that action, she encountered the serpent, I mean the Old Serpent. David, in like manner, had been scheduled to go to war, choosing to stay home, allowing his soldiers to go without all clearly in leadership with them (2 Samuel 11). Because he was outside of his divine position, his wandering eyes observed a naked woman bathing, and before long, his action had grave outcomes both in the immediate future as well as in the long term.

The object of his fancy, Bathsheba, lost her husband on the battlefield, premeditatedly; a child from that encounter was born outside the glory of God and died; and David was left to deal with a fallout that went beyond his imagination. Believers are blessed to have gotten Psalm 51 out of David's strong knowledge of God, heartfelt pain, grief, and repentance.

The glory of God that finds us in our mess has made it possible for us all, by David, to have the glorious words of forgiveness in Psalm 51 for our use. Whenever we offend Him and have the awareness to yield our members in humility for mercy, our loving God forgives us.

Eve met the snake in the garden. She became engaged in a conversation she ought not have, for unbeknownst to her, the snake was not her old familiar friend but Satan. The Old Serpent spoke with Eve:

> And he said unto the woman, Yea, hath God said, Ye shall not eat of every tree of the garden?[2] And the woman said unto the serpent, We may eat of the fruit of the trees of the garden:[3] But of the fruit of the tree which is in the midst of the garden, God hath said, Ye shall not eat of it, neither shall ye touch it, lest ye die.[4] And the serpent said unto the woman, Ye shall not surely die:[5] For God doth know that in the day ye eat thereof, then your eyes shall be opened, and ye shall be as gods, knowing good and evil. (Genesis 3:1b–5).

They were already "gods," made in the image of God. Further, Adam's genealogy lists him as the son of God (Luke 3:38).

Eve was not the keeper of God's truth; Adam was. She was distracted. Many of us are easily distracted, and this has the potential to impact our lives, marriages, families, careers, churches, communities, and society at large. Eve proceeded to engage in an unholy conversation with the Old Serpent that resulted in the distortion of information, contamination of her mind, and their fall from grace. She missed the subtlety of his deception. Inevitably, she opened the door of lust of eye and the resultant disobedience.

Evening (and problems) arrived because Eve took on the role of Adam in both an ungodly and an unusual communication between good and evil. In doing so, victoriously, she usurped the power given to Adam in honor of his knowledge of God.

The Old Serpent caused Adam to place his wife, Eve, first in an attempt to shame God, Yahweh. Before they were separated, they were one flesh. By eating of the fruit because Eve gave it to him, though the Lord God had told them not to, he was letting Eve know they were of more importance to each other than God was to them. Blissfulness corrupted his thoughts in the same way that a woman can take over the role of her husband (giving in to her whims when he ought to stand his ground) in unusual situations because of blissfulness.

Easy to misinterpret in God's holy scriptures are the words "Therefore shall a man leave his father and his mother, and shall cleave unto his wife: and they shall be one flesh." (Genesis 2:24).

Husbands have often fallen prey to their wives' subtle influences and domination. Some more easily would push aside parents whom they have loved and honored if a wife's anger would be kindled if they were to show an ounce of love and care toward these parents. A wife's subtle claim of "You're too close to your parents" can be seen as a clue for the husband to stay away from his parents or the entire family, to prove he is his own person (man). But nowhere in his demonstration of love (gracious light) and care of parents/extended family is his person challenged.

To keep ungodly peace in the home, the husband follows his wife in contradicting God's law, requiring us to honor our father and mother. (Adam too failed to honor God in the garden.) The husband is now joined with her in selfishness, dishonor, bitterness of her heart, greed (death of love in the heart), and in disobedience to mankind's honor of God.

That fruit had been there all along and had generated no interest in Eve's mind. Suddenly she lusted for the fruit, ate it, and became a tool for the Old Serpent to get Adam to eat what he was not supposed to eat. "And when the woman saw that the tree was good for food, and that it was pleasant to the eyes, and a tree to be desired to make one wise, she took of the fruit thereof, and did eat, and gave also unto her husband with her; and he did eat" (Genesis 3:6).

To honor Eve instead of God, Adam moved from the presence of God and ate with Eve. How many times have we dragged others into our distorted views of things?

I shudder to think that eating a piece of apple with my husband (siding with him against a request or instruction from God) could have such far-reaching implications.

Eve might have said something poignant that allowed him to dishonor God so easily, and mankind lives on to pay the price. We left the presence of the holy God to be dominated by an unholy adversary, but for the mercy of God.

The Bible says their eyes were opened. So we ask: what they were opened to and for what reason? Did they not have far better opened eyes and vision prior to that moment of the fall? Their eyes saw God. How blind can one be if his or her eyes see our loving God? But the eyes of Adam and Eve that were supposedly opened now only made them aware of their nakedness (humanity), which was previously covered by light. They were aware of their failed state, lack of knowledge, death, foolishness, and burial (eternal life without God in it).

They heard the voice of God in the garden. They experienced the goodness of being with God, without an ounce of what they would come to know as fear, because they were in God's presence. It reminds me of Satan, who had become ashes, or darkness. They were better with God, and so are we. All had changed for them.

They were now naked, with "supposed" eyes opened. They were naked, and carnality had stepped in. Their atmosphere was now one of darkness. Heaven above them had closed, and the glory of God's covering over them was waning. Adam would blame Eve for their troubles, but he had left her essentially unprotected. A new reality was beginning to emerge. Lord God, the light that covered their nakedness, had left unusually quietly.

We struggle today to see and hear God because of disobedience. In the serious beginning of mankind, seeing and hearing God was ours to enjoy. Satan ensured Adam and Eve did not stay (remain protected) in the old glory.

Adam and Eve were still God's. He punishes, but He never forgets His own. God's loving mercy and compassion roused God's protective self. God Himself stood to protect them, for Adam had covered them with (perishable) leaves. By covering them with leaves, Adam was saying, "We are going to be going back to the earth from which we came."

Our Master Holy Spirit said the killing of the animal to cover Adam and Eve was an expression that acknowledged they were now a wounded couple (i.e., separated from God). But our Lord Jesus Christ would offer Himself as the true substitutional sacrifice that would return mankind to God.

God is love. He had given Adam a mouth to declare and establish things, love, gladness, peace, and power to dominate, but not fear. However, after Adam and Eve sinned, they experienced fearfulness—an attribute of the Old Serpent. In his lowly state, Adam's heart had taken on the personality of the Old Serpent, blaming God for his troubles (vileness) and further disconnecting himself from God.

The woman God birthed from his rib, the beauty that once wowed him, was now his badge of insult to God. In nakedness and lacking true knowledge or illumination that he was still a child of God, he blamed Eve, whose frailty he shifted to be God's, though it was Satan's. But it was the Old Serpent, the ungodly impersonator now inside Adam's heart, who spoke, for God was no longer in their hearts.

We know that embedded in her name, "Eve," and structure, there remained the mystery of mankind returning to God. When God asked Eve what she had done, Eve did not blame Adam, argue, or lie to God. She placed the blame squarely on the wicked one, the Old Serpent.

Separation from God had opened Eve's inner eyes, though Adam's had now closed. Our Eve's generations would birth the immortal man (our Lord Jesus Christ), lovingly in the future.

Eve, fallen, still demonstrated she knew that the special and glorious honor of creation belongs to God. She gave God a "laced with love" response, letting Him know it was the Old Serpent who was the culprit. Though He was angry, this must have pleased God. Eve responded to God in worship, bringing women to God a sacrifice of worship and praise of God, the great creator, Father, and life giver.

Evening was around, but the light inside Eve still shone supreme. It will be seen one day, within time. Eve followed Adam out of the Garden of Eden to a lesser place, closing the gate of heaven against her and her husband. Yet there was a Seed to be planted, and God had the Seed. This meant Adam was still connected to God, because God needed a womb in which to plant the Promised Seed, and Eve and her generation had a womb for the planting of the Seed.

God was still with them, unbeknownst to Adam and Eve. He was with Adam and Eve spiritually but must fulfill the law of possession of the earth. Eve, prone to wander, could have wandered off again. She was cornered by Satan, the Old Serpent, who had been studying and mapping her behavior patterns. He didn't just show up to ask her those nonsensical questions. He meant to destroy Eve, who was to multiply and populate the earth and who in her womb (her generation) already carried the secret (a womb) to dominion over the earth. Her sub-gate, her womb, was the target. By going with Adam, Eve gave God a chance to grant Adam his salvation, redeeming him through the birth of our Lord Jesus Christ.

Eve remained a woman after God's heart. He did not disown Eve, despite her gross error; nor did He disown Adam for failing to ensure they stayed within His presence. God made sure they did not remain fallen for all eternity. God protected the Tree of Life by lovingly placing Cherubs as watchers, giving Adam and Eve a chance at repentance, by Himself, through our Lord Jesus Christ.

CHAPTER 5

The Cooperative Praise of Rahab: Giving God Her Worse for God's Better

We truly never know what each day will bring into our lives. I always say to my husband, "Every day is a miracle, a blessing." The holy Word says God daily loads us with benefits. Yet we often don't notice these blessings; many of them are unseen.

We may think these benefits are not occurring, but they are if we see life in general as the exceptional gift of God that it is. Whether we are just surviving or earnestly thriving, life itself is a gift, and the living alone have the chance to change their circumstances, with God's help, even if through other people.

It follows, then, that the glorious promises of God are for the living, as they can still pray for God's intervention, love, inquire of the Lord, cry, stand, give, bless, plan, live, possess, sustain, create, guide, rise, praise, hope, worship, rest, clean up messes, rejoice, move the Old Serpent out of their lives, and much more.

There are benefits that are happening in our lives that we fail to identify or recognize because they are not what Adanne Mercy Ebere calls "jumbo jets landing at your roof-top" blessings from God. Each day, you miss the airplane of wisdom that moved next door to you (e.g., a great idea for saving your marriage, good insight on an upcoming decision, a good friend sent by God who stopped by to help change the atmosphere around your home, or Lord God's awesomeness in the form of a salary raise).

Two strangers came to Rahab's house, needing information on how to cross over Jericho to the Promised Land. Her house was just a room in the Jericho wall for a lost one. Yet, unbeknownst to her seemingly disjointed life, the covering of God was on her.

The Jericho wall, a position of security and help, served to bring Rahab into contact with the people who would rescue her from her world condition (i.e., prostitution). What you are lovingly going to be in life—opportunities—is part of the suddenness of your life. This wayward daughter seemingly knew the loving God of the people who were outside her room on the wall, which could have been destroyed at any moment, asking for help.

Rahab had a visitation from two spies Joshua had sent to scout Jericho, a fortified city. Its wall prevented them from reaching the land God had promised to give the descendants of Abraham, their patriarch, and a good friend of God.

Enslavement for 430 years in Egypt delayed Israel's arrival at Canaan. This was the land God had promised Abraham's descendants would occupy at the right time. Israel was now thirty years behind in possessing this land, and the key to getting there was to bring down the walls of Jericho.

The wall prevented Israel from cooperating with God's plans for its nation. People do not go through walls, as only our Savior Jesus did after His resurrection when His disciples were gathered for dinner, doubting whether it was their Lord that they had seen.

But God, who is full of mercy and kindness and who calls us to fulfill purposes, had called Rahab, unbeknownst to Abraham's children, to help get them to the land God had promised their ancestor. Israel would need God's help going through Jericho's wall, and He would offer them help in a divine way.

Rahab's house was inside one of Jericho's protective walls. Those walls signified the greatness of the land of Jericho, and the gate nearest to her house, which was open at the time, was the entrance through which the spies (goodness) came into her life.

Their visit moved Rahab from a place of cruelty to a place of love in God. Joshua's two spies from Shittim were then symbolic of the two thieves crucified next to our Lord Jesus Christ at Calvary, one of whom was moved from a place of cruelty to a place of love in the process.

When the spies entered the home of Rahab, the fact that only two were sent (to confer life where death had found expression) lets us know there is spiritual symbolism to Joshua's decision, for God was leading and guiding him.

Here there was an agreement between God and humanity in the person of Joshua. The Old Serpent took away the covering of Adam and Eve, bringing them into disagreement with God, but Joshua, in the similitude of our Lord Jesus Christ, in obedience, would align with God's will for His children to return them to the Promised Land. Joshua would move with divine guidance and help to possess a land promised to God's people, returning them to their rightful place.

The two spies who went to Rahab signify a win for mankind over the great deception of Satan. Mankind would begin their journey to eternal rest in God with the angelic pronouncement of the birth of our Lord Jesus Christ.

Rahab, unbeknownst to all, was divinely positioned on one of the walls of Jericho. She, who was begrimed, now had a strong granting of divine honor. It goes that the sex that occupied her life gave way to the loving gift of a positional marriage to one of Israel's men (a servant of God), initiating mankind's salvation.

Rahab was in the center of Israel's move to the Promised Land. Ironically, among other things, Israel sought to serve other gods, for its people moved from worship of God to the worship of gods of other lands, including Moab.

Living in a low position in life (of sort) was chosen to be a part of the foundation of our Lord Jesus's birth, life, death, and resurrection. Rahab believed in the God of Israel, and she did not fit the mold her society had created. Her warring against her god and going after the God of Israel means she goaded her nation's god. It was her trust and belief in the Living God of Israel that brought her liberation.

Equipped with information from Rahab, and with directions from God, for six days Israel marched quietly around the City of Jericho; seven priests bearing the ark and trumpets of rams' horns led the march around Jericho's city walls. On the seventh day, they encompassed the city seven times. The priests blew the trumpets, the people gave a loud shout, and the wall of Jericho fell flat into the ground, as though it had never been there.

Rahab, who believed in God, and her family went with Israel to the Promised Land. This lowly daughter of Eve, key to the walls of Jericho coming down, helped fallen man to rise to their glorious position, moving them toward reconciliation with God.

You may never know from where your help will come. Do not despise your humble beginnings, but remain in God's awesome presence. Awful things can become valued treasures. Israel, by selecting Rahab for marriage, caused the graven images among them to fall, giving birth to the great David, the worshipper, whose lineage gave birth to our Lord Jesus Christ.

Hebrews 11:31 lets us know that, through faith, the notorious sinner Rahab did not perish along with the disobedient, for she had welcomed the spies and sheltered them. She changed position. Her family changed location, and it benefited her more than she would know, allowing Gentiles to be a part of God's kingdom.

The word "harlot" denotes mankind's weakness, unbelief, and fall. It had moved Israel into enmity with God. Repeatedly in scriptures, God reminds Israel that they were going between Him and other gods. We see both the weakness and the goodness of humans in the kindness of the peculiar Rahab.

We are reminded by Apostle James that we are justified not just by faith, but also by our works, such as lowly Rahab offered God. Israel was moving toward her final place of settlement, the Promised Land, where the Canaanites, Gentiles, and Israelites will again be unified to begin a divine journey with help from a generation of Eve—wayward Rahab.

Rahab brought quite a lot to our attention. I asked our Master Hoy Spirit what lessons we should derive from the Rahab story. I hadn't truly thought about the actual benefit of her inclusion, beyond the obvious that our Lord God chose the lowly things of this world to confound the wise and the rich.

The Master Holy Spirit brought to my attention that, when a woman gives birth, she truly doesn't have full knowledge of whom she has birthed.

It is from the dunghill that God raises His glorious children, for our bad may be good to God. Perhaps a friend redirected Rahab's purpose. Poverty and its attendant outcomes, sickness, low self-esteem, and more perhaps added to her woes. Still, a wounding of sorts may have pushed her over the edge, causing her to veer off.

The mother of Rahab did not know Rahab was going to be a grimed girl. She might have taken care of her just the way we too would take care of our beloved daughters. But somewhere along the journey of life, the road turned.

A friend of a friend changed who she was and made herself weakened in the knee, for on the night before her wedding, she had found her fiancé in bed with another woman.

Rahab, for whatever the reason, was not birthed with the assignment of becoming graceless, unless the Lord God had a specific assignment for her that mimicked Israel's awkward relationship with God.

Our Master Holy Spirit says we are never to give up on our children. We can imagine what Rahab's family may have thought of her—how they may have ostracized, hated, and mocked her at family gatherings, or never even invited her to any. But it was this strange creature, who was not worth having around, who saved them.

The problem emerges when we fail to go on our knees and pray, seeking God's face to change our children's lives where they are floundering, for many of their battles have spiritual underpinnings. Rahab must have been on her knees (a posture of contrition), praying unendingly for her own deliverance.

Many heard about Israel's divinely guided conquests. But only Rahab keyed into the significance of their warrior exploits, which to her brought thoughts of victory over her unusual circumstances.

We know, from the time our children are in the womb, Satan comes after them to derail their destinies. God lets us know that every child is easily a winner of souls; victoriously, courageously, Old Serpent's nemesis; and a laborer for God. These virtues make them targets of Satan who comes to kill, steal, and destroy. Thus, if we get stuck on the cuteness of our children as infants, our children may be doomed. Our Lord Jesus Christ, beloved of the Father, came to give us abundant life, even eternal life with Him. He lets us know to not relent in our fight to preserve the lives of our children. His loving sacrifice on the Cross of Calvary has won battles against Satan for us.

Our children are meant to protect us by standing guard at gates (places of import, points of vulnerabilities in parents' lives, and the like), not to be victims of Satan who is bent on seriously destroying them. Rahab was one such child, but God found her.

We must not relent in praying for our children, seeking the face of God for them and trusting the Holy Spirit of God for their safety. So if our children should become schoolteachers (molding young minds toward goodness and greatness) or lawyers (liberating innocent ones from unlawful imprisonment, spiritually and unduly), or make other career choices, all will be done to the glorification of God.

It was no accident that Joshua's spies ended up at Rahab's. They were divinely guided. May the feet of our children be divinely guided as well. Molding our children begins from the womb, for God lets us know He called some prophets while they were yet in their mothers' wombs.

God initiates a purpose-filled conversation with every one of us, even from the womb, even while we are still very young. We should not abandon those we feel don't measure up. Rahab was one of those "carefully gifted" children; in her future was salvation.

Prophet Bentil shared with me that as a child he left his relatively well-to-do family and moved into the home of a very poor family. He was drawn to their loving nature; the parents lovingly took care of the children, though they were extremely poor. Everyone went to a farm a long distance away to either plant or harvest the produce they would eat to sustain themselves.

Later in life, he understood God's divine preparation for his prophetic ministry. In the foundation of that family were issues causing poverty (of mind and resources), lack, and inopportunity. It was a gifted little boy (the upcoming Prophet Nana Bentil), unbeknownst to them, our Master Holy Ghost had used to disconnect the family from their foundational problems, by his presence in their family. It was like God using the little shepherd boy David to slay Goliath.

By the power of the Holy Spirit, we can stand to fight for the children and rescue them from the hands of the evil one. Parents' hearts must be yielded to God so He can use their children someday to be His weapon against wickedness in families and in the larger society.

David, in the wilderness with his father's sheep, and alone with God, slayed the bear and lion that came after his sheep. In these moments, David might have thought he was only being a brave shepherd. This is similar to our Lord Jesus Christ, the Good Shepherd, who would lay down His life for His sheep. What Rahab's great-great-grandson, David, didn't know at the time was that he was learning, in secret, how to be a king and a carrier of the divine presence of God. What his great-great-grandmother, Rahab, too didn't know was that, though a prostitute, she was ideally chosen by God to lay the foundation for the soon-coming King's birth and ministry of reconciliation.

David's killing of Goliath using skills gained through God's presence in the wilderness while tending his father's sheep would be showcased in public and would help him to rule Israel at the appointed time. Lowly Rahab gave us this David, a great man.

I would like to call attention to a problem I have observed that may help explain why this favorite daughter of God is added.

Rahab accommodated strangers, and her life, her family's lives, and our lives are also changed by her kindness. She entertained two strangers; encouraged a nation, ensuring they stayed with God's plans for them to take on the land of Jericho; saved her family from destruction; followed her new nation; married one of them by divine guidance; and became the mother of the root of Jesse. Our Lord Jesus Christ is birthed from her lineage, and our salvation is won.

Rahab moved from prostitute to wife. She came to Israel and helped the people lay the foundation for our salvation. Some young people come into our families, and our families are destroyed by the spirit in them through witchcraft, wickedness, greed, insecurity, manipulation, fear, low self-esteem, lack of fear of God, and much more. Many young people have a hard time accommodating the people they know, especially in-laws, thwarting God's plans. Yet it is our hope that we will witness these same ones, in the future, achieving great things.

Disregard of in-laws may be one-sided. The perpetrator in the marriage, the one with the unholy power, usually maintains strong ties with his or her parents, but that kindness is not afforded his or her spouse's parents. Yet we are always to lovingly work with God, as our cooperative mother Rahab showed us and did so splendidly.

Genesis 2:24 says, "Therefore shall a man leave his father and his mother and shall cleave unto his wife: and they shall be one flesh."

This is a very easy scripture to be misunderstood, as seen earlier in this book. This part of the scripture is lovingly misheard: "and shall cleave unto his wife: and they shall be one flesh."

Please, let's examine this scripture:

"and shall cleave": (i.e., become one to another a joy, emboldened and wealthy, and to occupy the land; God was to find a help meet for Adam)

"unto his wife": (i.e., wife and husband are now united as one flesh before God; the couple is now united to perpetuate the lineage)

"and they": (i.e., the son, and the parents' loving new daughter-in-law)

"shall be": (i.e., are to be coupled in truth, to "sustain the new generation")

"one": (i.e., together under the covering of Yahweh, God Almighty)

"flesh": (i.e., to give them a man or woman to cover, and elevate, God's children)

If a son leaves his mother and father's house (covering) to find a wife, it is as though he is going out hunting to return with a good catch, a new daughter for his parents. While the son now has an important responsibility and must accord priority to his wife, he is not to ignore his parents, and the family.

The combination of the two under the covering of parents, whether they be dead or alive, courageously returns the family unit to God (goodness).

Eve was to ensure Adam remained under God's courageous covering as we would today under our parents.

Parents are not to direct what happens in their son's new family but are to manage the generation from a social distance to ensure they are settled, established, thriving, among other things. In this way, we honor God as people of faith who pass on family histories, break family curses, share wisdom with the young ones, and reveal secrets to building a successful marriage, even if parents have failed in their own marriages.

Parents get to courageously enjoy the couple and the grandchildren (if lovingly there), under God's covering. But imagine if the new daughter the son brings home with him does not join with him in truth.

Eve was hidden in Adam when he was created, only to be separated and rejoined as one flesh in marriage. The gift of union is important to God. The plan by dubious individuals is causing the words "becoming one flesh" to refer to causing one partner to melt and disappear into the other and no longer exist as an independent voice. A woman I know had not had her parents visit her family in thirty years because her husband boldly had not deemed them suitable visitors. This is the wickedness of Satan, whether it is the man or the woman who is the progenitor of such an unholy lifestyle.

Women have special gifts to sustain the family. These include the fruits of the spirit and their expansion, enveloped in love, such as peace and gladness in stormy situations, patience during trials, the ability to endure, wisdom to cushion spouses, the joyful raising of the children, faith and trust in God amid delays, and much more.

Causing a woman to lose virtue, her place in the family, and her God-given wisdom and knowledge could result in a great fall for both the man and the woman and may cause the family to experience many defeats.

The wisdom in the man and the woman should bring them to God. If the woman should usurp the man's gifts, including being the head of household (holy), she too seeks to derail generations yet unborn.

Any woman who is not allowed to share her special gifts may not pour lovingly into the lives of her children, spouse, and others. For the man, deep darkness in the form of sadness, silent rage, angry outbursts, rudeness, loneliness, insecurity, and more may abound where love and kindness should have found abode.

A husband may seek to harness the wisdom of his wife, including her financial acumen and better ability in dealing with personal household matters, making her responsible for aspects of the marriage in which he may be lacking. It may vary in families, but when there is a problem, it releases only "soft confusion" and shouting of sorts, with God as the winning referee. Not much can go wrong then.

Wearing (owning) a ring does not negate the fact that the two still belong to their families; they must not abandon them, just as they must not abandon their God. The reality is that these young people may come from families that are broken, meaning that leaving those families behind may be much easier to do. But you cannot outrun your shadow; it may cause you to drag the wrong action (spirit) into your home. If a daughter-in-law's goal is to not like the family she came into, generations suffer. Our sons coming from afar, and our daughters nursed at your side, as noted in Isaiah 60:4c, reminds us that our sons bring us wives to uphold our families (my family, and your family).

When one dislikes or maltreats in-laws, wickedness has found a home in that family. Evil (wickedness) has nothing good about it, and it is dark (and lonely). It has the potential of breeding jealousy, disunity, abuse, poverty, disfavor, rebellion, hatred, greed, and more. God's righteous ones can do nothing but pray.

Parents are not always kind to their new daughters-in-law, but the wisdom of the Ancient (God) must be brought to bear to save the family unit.

Lord Jesus Christ, the Master Holy Spirit, thank You for all You do for us to uphold our families. We gratefully bow our loving hearts in praise, worship, and adoration of You, great God.

The union of husband and wife in the spiritual realm is a strong force against evil, as they are jointly honoring Yahweh, Lord Jesus Christ, by preserving the integrity of the family unit for generations to come. But marital union can bring the Old Serpent, the devil, barreling down on the couple to destroy them, sowing discord, confusion, creating conflicts, producing loneliness, and even causing divorce.

The victorious covering of a parent is a powerful force against the Old Serpent's onslaughts. Therefore, parents are needed to help protect the couple to secure the next generation. The wife must blend the two families lovingly together since they are to birth the next generation. I am aware that not all couples desire having children. This is now a personal decision. God's plan for Adam and Eve was to be fruitful and multiply (lovingly bear children, grow spiritually, wonderfully fulfill purpose, and produce grain). Some still experience difficulties having children. We ask the Lord to lovingly intervene [quickly] in such cases.

Couples can be manipulated into living in fear of losing their partners. Thus, insecurity can become a very destructive force or power and a curse to these unions. However, confidence, boldness, gratitude, giving to others, and knowledge of our loving God are great antidotes to the feeling of insecurity in a marriage.

In addition to one partner feeling insecure in a marriage, parents, for whatever reason, can feel wounded when their son or daughter gets married. This too can be destructive (through hatred and jealousy toward their child's spouse). We know, then, that it is important for the union to give honor where honor is due, among other things.

As we revisit great-grandmother Rahab, we know our wayward daughters must never be excluded from our lives. A not-so-beloved family member, Rahab, not only saved her family from destruction, but also became an important link in the ancestral lineage of our Lord Jesus Christ. A look at the genealogy of our Savior and Lord Jesus Christ shows us where Rahab appears in the lineage of Jesus (Matthew 1).

Women working lovingly with God know that such work is not always about their needs or feelings in the moment; sometimes it is about goodness towards others. We try to love even the wayward ones in our families in celebration of God's love for and mercy toward us all.

While we were yet sinners, our Lord Jesus died for us. As Mother Rahab has shown us lovingly, kings and queens are known to come from the not-so-greats among us.

CHAPTER 6

Ruth And Hannah's Eyes: Winning God's Heart

Esau (who married a Gentile wife) and Jacob's (who married two sisters from his mother's golden family), servant of God, winning rivalry would be settled partly because God found a faithful carrier of a divine Seed.

We've all heard of a Moabite, Ruth, wife of Boaz, who though joined in pain with her mother-in-law, Naomi, set aside her own fears to go back with Naomi to her home country. Her reversed loyalty would help close the gap between Esau and Jacob, two wounded brothers of old.

Though married for nearly ten years with no children of her own, by divine selection, Ruth remarried and became the mother of Obed. Obed was the father of Jesse, and Jesse the father of God's special friend King David. Jesse had no name in Israel but for the name of "the Root of Jesse" that David brought him, a powerful name that is associated with our Lord Jesus Christ. Boaz too would be missing in the genealogy but for the grace of Ruth.

Early in 1 Samuel 1, Hannah in pain and drenched in tears, in dire need of her own children—a pain commonly faced today by many who ache to have children. The "cunning" love of a doting husband who already had children by his other wife could not console Hannah; neither could her being married to this wealthy man replace the emptiness in both her heart and her womb.

Two worlds would come together in the not-so-distant future, as God had set apart Hannah's womb, unknown to her, to birth God's prophet for the nation of Israel, His chosen nation. We find both Ruth and Hannah, differing in perspectives, uplifted eventually by God who answers His children. Let us look at what it is about these women that can help us today.

I laughed at the thought of hearing my late mother-in-law Oluremilekun's adage, which she often said to her children: "When you cry, you must see." This wise woman was telling her children, for example, that their being in despair is not a reason for them to cross the road without looking out for oncoming cars; being in tears is not an excuse for getting hit by a car. She was simply saying that crying, sadness, fear, and sorrow must not lessen one's wisdom and understanding amid difficult situations but that one must look unto God for solutions. She was a devoted Christian and a pourer of God's jointly loving help to His needy ones.

Borne from an awareness of their ungodly circumstances, Ruth and Hannah recognized the superiority of God over all situations, including those the Old Serpent had created to derail God's purposes in their lives. Among other things, by acknowledging the blessedness of God, these two women attracted God's attention to their situations. Let's see how they did it.

In 1 Samuel 1, the scriptures tell us that there was a certain man from Ramathaim, in the hill country of Ephraim, whose name was Elkanah. Google.com has enabled me to gain added insights into the woman Hannah and the circumstances surrounding the background in which she was married. The foundation problems or blessings of her husband's lineage help us better understand who she is.

Hannah's husband, Elkanah, was of the tribe of Levi. His name means "God has acquired" (https:// HYPERLINK "http://www.abarim-publications.com/" www.abarim-publications.com/Meaning/Elkanah.html) or "God has purchased" (https://www.name-doctor.com/name-elkanah-meaning-of-elkanah-27962.html, https:// HYPERLINK "http://www.thebump.com/" www.thebump.com›elkanah-baby-name).

Our Master Holy Spirit brought to my attention that Elkanah's name is akin to "one who was sold for naught and God bought him with His Blood." It lovingly reminds me of what happened to us believers as we lost our crown of glory in the Garden of Eden to the Old Serpent, but our Lord Jesus Christ bought us back with His own blood.

Of the women examined in this book, it would seem all of them, somehow, are wandering between tribes (children of great importance to God). We are all controlled by the mighty hand of God, whether we know, accept, and believe it or not.

The name "Levi," given to both one of Jacob's twelve sons and a tribe in Israel, means "united," "joined," or, sometimes, "joined in harmony" HYPERLINK "(https://www.verywellfamily.com/levi-name-meaning-or%20igin-" (https://www.verywellfamily.com/levi-name-meaning-or igin-popularity-5180368).

Our Master Holy Spirit noted that "joined in harmony" reflected the fact that evil (would-be human frailty) was joined with good (goodness of God to save His own) in the family of Jacob (the supplanter) to lovingly form a tribe in Israel. He added the name "Levi" to also mean "whatever is wrong with me will not overwhelm me." Our loving God saw to it that the evil in the family did not destroy His beloved Israelites (Jacob).

Elkanah was the son of Jeroham whose name means "cherished" or "one who finds mercy" (https://en.wikipedia.org/wiki/Jeroham#:~:text=Jeroham). The naming of this child as "one who obtains mercy" gives the impression that his parents encountered challenges with his birth.

Elkanah's grandfather was Elihu. The name Elihu calls our attention to the deep-seated love for God found in Elkanah's family. Elihu means "He is my God" (i.e., "My God is the only true God") (https:// www.jewishencyclopedia.com/articles/5633-elihu).

Our attention is on the fact that God instructs and teaches people knowledge. My take is that God was searching in this family for one who would be an instructor for His people and who would teach them new knowledge about who He is.

As we continue to examine his lineage, we find a name that calls our attention to the barrenness that was hidden in the family that Hannah had married into.

I was once rejected by the mother of a boy I had just met and who wanted to marry me. He went home the day I met him to tell his mother that he had met the love of his life. The mother rejected his choice without having met me.

When I shared the rejection with my own mother, she laughed. She said, "We wouldn't have let you marry him anyway, because his grandfather was lovingly known to have stolen somebody's chicken." It seems the boy's lineage was known for stealing. The young man has married multiple times since that encounter and is struggling still to find a right home for his marital rest.

Many women marry for love, not knowing anything about the men they're marrying or have married, lacking insight as to what is in their foundation; the evil or good hidden in one's foundation may follow generations forward, even those yet unborn.

Elihu was the son of Tohu, meaning "confusion, or emptiness: wasteness, that which is laid waste, desert; emptiness, vanity; nothing" (https://en.wikipedia.org/wiki/Tohu wa-bohu#:~:text).

I got very hopeful looking at Elkanah's lineage, partly because in him whose name denotes emptiness and wasteness lay the mystery of Samuel. Hiding in his genealogy is God's call for someone who would serve as a covering or watchman over Israel, His chosen people.

Elkanah's great-great-great-grandfather was Zuph. A few translations of the name increase our understanding. The name

"Zuph" means "honeycomb" (https://en.wikipedia.org›wiki›Zuph) and is a reference to dripping with honey (https:// HYPERLINK "http://www/" www. truthunity.net/mbd/zuph).

A closer look at Abarim Publications' translation reveals that it includes the verb "sapa," and they explain the name Zuph this way: "Speaks of covering, whether a literal covering of an item with an overlay like gold or the figurative covering of watchman's surroundings by his watchful gaze" (https://www.abarim-publications.com/Meaning/Zuph.html). Other sources indicate the name also means "beholds, observes, watches, roof, covering" (https:// HYPERLINK "http://www.sheknows.com/baby-names/name/zuph/)" www.sheknows.com/baby-names/name/zuph/).

How does a family go from emptiness to having a "watcher," a covering for its generation? Elkanah was married to two wives and had children by the second wife. Hannah was the first of Elkanah's two wives; the second was named Peninnah. Hannah had no children, while Peninnah had six sons and daughters.

We are not told the names of Peninnah's sons. We presupposed then that the covering was not yet born, as names are of great import to God's anointed people. Perhaps another generation is set to have him.

Part of Elkanah's family's ritual was the annual visit and worship at Shiloh where Hophni and Phinehas, the two sons of Eli, were priests of the Lord. To worship at Shiloh was to offer sacrifices to God. Elkanah would sacrifice animals and would give the bigger portions not to Peninnah (an unauthorized woman who took Hannah's position to produce an heir for her beloved husband) and her children but to the lone Hannah who had no real use for anything more than a small portion for an empty woman. To Hannah, her husband's material wealth and romantic gestures meant nothing when those who would enjoy them the most, children, were not yet born and may never be.

Hannah had a pattern of going to the temple year after year, petitioning God for a child and not having her prayers answered. As a believer of God's unfailing grace and mercy, she persisted. Elkanah loved her, but God had closed her womb. The Old Serpent, Peninnah, and her children were controlling Hannah's home.

In everything, glorify God. Hannah feared the Lord. She knew it was God who was to be blamed for her barrenness, so her knees remained bent before Him, hoping He would relent.

Peculiar to some humans is the tendency to abuse those who have no children, regardless of the reason for the lack. A friend of mine said that his wife was abused a lot because she couldn't have children and that he was told he had married a man instead of a woman because she was barren. This anointed man of God ended up having three children, honoring God. God knows how to play catch-up, seriously undermining the diabolical plans of the Old Serpent.

When I visited a local hospital in Cameroon as part of my doctoral studies, I encountered a woman with ten children who was admitted to the hospital. I asked why she had so many children, as she was suffering from uterine prolapse. She told me her former in-laws had driven her out of her marriage for being barren. When she met her current husband, God opened her womb. She began having children; one after the other they came. There was no end to the number of children God was willing to give her for the shame she had experienced, and for her part, she had no interest in stopping. She had just given birth to her tenth child.

Peninnah would provoke Hannah whose womb God had closed for reasons known only to Him. A story of an exceptional case was told of a very kind but barren woman who took care of the neighborhood kids. The story goes that one night, in a dream, God took her on a tour of a house and showed her many girls and boys who were her children, but God had decided otherwise.

She woke up from that dream knowing she was divinely protected by our loving God, and she appreciated her great victory, as she called it. Many of her town's children found her home the place to be when they were idle, hungry, or felt alone. Being there provided a golden opportunity to play, eat, or converse with other children. She was neither taunted nor ostracized in a society where not being able to conceive meant one was not really a woman.

Taunting a woman for the inability to bear children is not what our loving God expect of us. Gracious and compassionate is our God. Peninnah was envious of Hannah who, though barren, was loved tremendously by their husband. For years Peninnah taunted Hannah until she would weep and not eat.

A woman told me she would rather have a miscarriage than be childless without any indication she has the capacity to carry a child. Her choice, she said, was because she was tired of being called a man. God is God, after ten years of marriage, she had a daughter.

Another woman who also wanted a child badly would wear bundled-up clothing under her outfit daily to let her in-laws, neighbors, and friends know she had gotten pregnant—that she was a woman. The taunting from her countrymen had gotten to her after five years of marriage. Every seven months after that, she would ask her husband to relocate to another city to prevent being asked when she was due and about the baby.

One day, in deep abiding sorrow from the loss of her precious father and a husband who wanted time with his wife, her situation was elevated. She closed her eyes, opened up, and indulged. The focus on the loss of her dear father was great as she remembered the blessed gift of the wonderful dad the Almighty God had given her and her siblings. The one man she loved the most was gone, and having a baby seemed no longer a dire need.

The adjustment in mindset left her living from a place of gratitude to a kind and loving God, which overrode the fears and lies the Old Serpent had woven into her womb. Love entered her womb, the Old Serpent was squeezed out, and a good pregnancy followed! She had four children in all. When we taunt others, we are demonstrating the same pride and arrogance that Satan displayed before he was thrown out of heaven.

If we see our lives chiefly from the perspective of conceiving and giving birth, of having a doting husband, or of barrenness we may be experiencing in any area of our lives, it is a sort of distortion of God. We know no human condition is outside of God's capacity to change; even if no child is forthcoming, there's always a resolute joy and gladness in such homes.

There are many blessings in our lives that should occupy us daily, including the hope of glorious living, because the possibility still exists that things can change.

Hannah received more taunts when they would go to the house of the Lord in Shiloh to offer sacrifices and worship to God. She may have been lovingly going to worship at Shiloh for years, praying the same prayer of "Give me, give me, or I will die of a troubled heart"—a potentially dismissive prayer.

Perhaps heaven was also saying to Hannah, "Where is God's supremacy in your prayer?" Tears do not necessarily move God if they come from a place of our yielding to the impossibility of things in our lives rather than from sowing the goodness of the all-knowing God's creative will. But tears that acknowledge our loving and glorious God's awesomeness, kindness, favor, grace, mercy, sovereignty, and supremacy surely invite heaven into our affairs. God lets us know that we have a High Priest who cares about us and our infirmities. Worship and praise to our Father and God brings Him down to receive our gifts of a thankful mouth. The Old Serpent must bow as the impossible becomes possible.

So Hannah's results had always been the same and her thoughts always in this direction: "Maybe next year God will answer me." That was a definite maybe.

We don't know how long her husband was married to her before he thought to marry Peninnah, the other who gave him children. We are to always trust God. Hannah's time of childbirth may have been waning, but God was still watching.

On one trip to Shiloh that brings Hannah to our attention, something was different, and there was going to be a definitive yes this time. In fact, in the similitude of honored Abraham, by the same time the following year there would be a different outcome, because

Hannah had tapped into the mystery of who our great God truly is, and it was right in front of her.

It is a woman's choice whether to have children, if God's divine plan agrees with her decision, as God's overwhelming heart of love gives His children free choice, and so personal decisions are honored, with some exceptions. I have seen people who promised never to have children but did so, not knowing they were having babies. When a woman chooses to have one but cannot or is unable to for any reason, however, the heart tends to know no end of sorrow and sadness.

Eli, the prophet of God, was getting old. There would be a need for a replacement prophet since Eli's two sons were unfit to take on the mantle.

On this trip to Shiloh, Hannah saw Eli, the priest of God, sitting by a post in the temple. Though in tears, she elevated her thoughts to see in Eli's posture the goodness, the greatness, and the strength of God to correct barrenness.

The meanings in the names of Elkanah's people were now taking shape in Hannah's life. The name "Elihu" was a foreshadowing of what was about to happen to Hannah. (Tohu and a breakthrough were looming.)

God would have for Himself a loving observer, a roof, a watcher to cover Israel. Hannah was saying her prayers. She was muttering things with such deep sorrow that Eli thought she was drunk and should not have come into the temple in that state.

As stated before, my late mother-in-law, Oluremilekun Ibitola Odeinde, was fond of the saying, "When you cry, you must see." It seemed Hannah understood this old saying. Though full of sorrow, before her was the handwriting of God for the beholding of a child, and she opened her teary eyes and saw!

Hovering over Hannah's atmosphere was a shocked heaven because her eyes had seen the glory of a loving God in the temple, unbeknownst to her, in her understanding of Prophet Eli's sitting near the temple post. Hannah knew it meant good and evil were at war, and goodness was about to win.

Eli, in need of a priest to take his place in watering the impending dryness that now foreshadowed his upcoming departure from the earth, leaned on the fallen post of God, as his own children were not fit to carry on the work of God. Eli was calling on heaven with a deep sadness.

Eli and Hannah, two people with a common goal, were in the same place (the temple, the presence of God), victims of not knowing God's plans for His people. A change was in the atmosphere! We are reminded that, where two or three of God's children are gathered, He is in their midst. Heaven had an army fighting for both Eli and Hannah. Hannah, who had been in tears earlier, now saw the unfolding of God's plans for Israel in the old man and the post and in his calling to God for help.

The deceiver had caused her to insistently believe her womb was accursed, as opposed to waiting for the appointed time.

Prophet Eli accused Hannah of coming into the temple drunk (an unauthorized atmosphere before God). She was mindful and was not offended. But the crown of alcohol provides euphoria, while the search for God offers the true euphoria of the spirit, the one that Hannah experienced that day. Her lips were moving, but no sound came out because the heart was groaning. She was asked by the priest of God whether she was drunk on alcohol.

This prophet of God could feel the euphoric change in the atmosphere with this strange woman in the temple. He thought she was drunk. What he missed in that moment was that our Master Holy Spirit heard wonderful vows and arrived to seal them.

You can imagine the heart cry that our Lord Jesus Christ cried when He saw all His disciples abandoning Him and heard the sound of the cock crowing. The priest of God, Eli, asked her to put the wine away. This was a woman in the temple, and she was being accused of something vain. Without knowing what she had done, Eli was cooperating in prayer with her to manifest the realities of heaven on earth (cooperation with God's plans).

The Old Serpent might have told Eli no one was coming to take over God's work from him. Doom and gloom? No! God was still watching! Hannah dried up her tears and became a place of prayer to move God to act in her favor. Prophetically, a shift into a joyous expectation in the sweet presence of God attracts a shift in the atmosphere and ushers one into the realm of earnest victory in our Lord Jesus Christ.

But Eli seemed to have found someone with whom to talk. Considering the weaknesses of his own two sons, he determined Hannah wasn't a local, and she didn't seem to be judging him. He talked lovingly. She wasn't drunk, but many others have been in her position and have had to drink, finding winning comfort in alcohol. How painful that must be to our loving God who, by His earnest and glorious will, knows how to transform sadness to the joy of love, which Yahweh does for those who drink from our Master Holy Spirit, the River of Life.

On this fateful day, Hannah moved from pleading for her own child—a selfish thought—to a sacrificial place of meeting an urgent need she could visually see that God had. Hannah's tears became worship and praise of God, and He was there to receive them.

Israel's patriarch, Abraham, had a covenant with God. He had promised to make him a father of many nations. This was said of a man who was old at the time and had not even one child. God gave Abraham a child, Isaac, and by that one, God proved to Abraham that He is a promise-keeping God. The eventual twelve tribes of Israel are from that one seed.

The sacred time in Prophet Eli's presence allowed Hannah to key into the promise-keeping God and bargain for herself. She received a son to cover Israel. Hannah would bring him back to God after he was weaned from the breast (from the closeness of earthly pleasures, to get him vying for heavenly glory).

My mom, loving Abigail, would say, "You should never owe God." We do so through the vows we make to Him. She would say, "You should allow God to owe you by His promises in His holy Word. He is a promise-keeping God, but we do not know when He's going to come for the vows that we make to Him." This special woman was speaking wisdom from the scripture, and she knew firsthand about vows, and obedience.

When we make vows to God, let's honor them immediately or at their appointed time. God is merciful and kind. His grace will help us do what is right. Let's revere Him by honoring our vows.

Hannah had made a vow to God, and she planned to fulfill her vow at the appointed time.

Hannah was barren and grieving inside, but the good of a loving prophet was hidden in her. Her husband's lineage hid wilderness and wastage, but it would take her to break them, placing over Israel the divine covering she needed and deserves.

Barrenness can occur in any area of our lives. It can take the form of a lack of social ties, chronic joblessness, major financial hardship, loveless marriages, grief over the loss of a spouse, and other such things. For Hannah, her barrenness was childlessness.

Her husband's great wealth could not mitigate her sorrow or resolve her barrenness without God's intervention. The fruit of a kept promise to God and blessings of accessing God's divine timing made Hannah not only a mother of a prophet, but also a mother of many other children.

God, patient in finding a prophet for His people, when evil (barrenness) and good (an unwavering determination to be of divine service to God) collided that day in the temple as a man of God made a prayer over a barren woman, helped open the door for this daughter of God.

Hannah broke the spell of barrenness by words spoken from a place of utter awareness, regard, knowledge, and understanding of God's momentous need for a prophet in the larger world and not in her personal one.

See God's Eli sitting near the post and try making a proclamation to God; give out a vow to God. All in all, it might be that He is waiting for someone to step in and meet His needs for humanity in this dispensation; in the way that you too can benefit from it.

Hannah's sacrifice called God's attention, promoting her into the supernatural, making her who was once barren and ordinary into the mother of a kingmaker.

We now know that while Eli was sitting and thinking of what comes next—for he was well advanced in age, and there were no good prospects for a prophet of God on the horizon—the heavens reopened and the covering cast over the nation moved. Hannah keyed in! The holy deed of exchange took place.

Hannah promised God a prophet, for she would offer her womb as a carrier of the God-loving prophet, and in exchange, she too would one day be called a mother. Hannah wanted nothing more, not even another child; just one would do.

Daily, we too must expect the unexpected. So when we are called to possess the gates of the enemy in any form, we too should be ready to say, "We are here Lord; choose us." Every day, a miracle happens. This seems to be such a casual statement and a cliché. But it gives us great comfort to believe in the miracle of life when one's life hits a speed bump on the road and the supernatural happens.

Adanne Mercy Ebere always says, "What can these little hands of mine do, Lord? The old laughter they are pouring on me is directed truly at You, my God. Father, intervene for me." She is saying, "I am Your seed of Abraham, and I have no power of my own. So, my God, fight for me."

Hannah too was asking God to fight Satan's will against her; what could her little womb do without God's intervention? The

Creator of the heavens and the earth has in His possession an unlimited store of love, grace, wisdom, miracles, favor, and overshadowing blessings for us.

Hannah left the temple that day in good spirits. She ate, worshipped God more the next day, and the family left for home. Hannah became pregnant, and by the following year, she had a son. The Giver of all good gifts had given her the son she asked for—a worker, a prophet for Israel. The name she gave him was Samuel, which means "God has heard" (https:// HYPERLINK "http://www.thebump.com/b/" www.thebump.com/b/ Samuel-baby-name). God's mantle for the spiritual grooming of Samuel was in his name.

She did not make the trip to Shiloh this time for a good reason: to wean the little boy that was called from birth to serve. Her job was done. Hannah was no longer the barren woman. Her husband's lineage had produced for God the covering He needed for Israel. Hannah had thought she was done having children. After all, all she wanted was one. She was a mother now and had kept her promise to God. She was no longer a laughingstock or the talk of the town—the rich man's barren wife. Hannah was a mother of a prophet of God—one that would be known throughout Israel to be among Israel's great prophets of God.

So Hannah prayed a long prayer in gratitude and praise of God, and she wonderfully described her victory over barrenness and its attendant problems. Peninnah's taunting and shaming that had made her life its abode, and even depression, was gone now. Living in Hannah's life now were the pleasures of a loving God.

The Lord is a rewarder of our labor of love. God blessed Hannah with more children for her sacrificial giving. When Hannah's children were growing up, it seemed Peninnah's were grown and gone out into the world. It was Peninnah who was now seemingly barren, for she did not have her children around to take care of her daily needs. Hannah's children had to help the one who had made fun of their mother. It is not where we start that matters but how and where we end up. Hannah prayed.

Ruth's life's promise would intercept Hannah's birth of Samuel, a prophet in the making. When our hearts' desires cry out to God, we are to be sure they do so for something that God can use.

Let's not desire the tall, handsome man when the purpose is for us to look accomplished to our families and friends. A great catch is one that has a heart that desires to become a better representation of God in your life, your family, and society at large.

Women work lovingly with God in many ways, engaging His presence to the betterment of the world in which they live, work, fellowship, and play. Ruth saw in the person of bereaved Naomi, her mother-in-law, the power of God shared in her heart: the love, honor, care, power, and wisdom of Naomi's God. Ruth, though freed from a barren relationship by the death of the husband of her youth, looked inward and made a decision that changed all their lives for good.

After the death of her husband and two sons, bereaved Naomi was willing to forge a new life without her daughters-in-law, Ruth and Orpah. Ruth, for her part, was willing to go where Naomi would go, staying anywhere with her, her people becoming hers too, and willing to die among Naomi's people.

Ruth's choice helped set on course the birth of our Lord Jesus and His finished work on the cross, among other things. Not all may subscribe to the life of good faith, trust in God, the love of God toward humans, wisdom to bring time into eternity, the belief in our Lord Jesus Christ, and Christ's finished work on the cross of Calvary, but we see all these through Ruth's sacrifice.

Ruth had learned from Naomi how to serve this God of stillness in times of unbearable storms. This little leaf of righteousness, Ruth, coming with love, helped to bring eternity, our Lord Jesus Christ, into time, His looming birth, crucifixion, and resurrection from the dead.

There is reward in doing and being good. For those who at times think generosity toward others is a curse, Ruth's choice to stay with Naomi instead of forging a new life for herself speaks volumes about the grace of kindness.

One might have thought to oneself, "Must one give up one's youth for an old woman's joy, one who has lived her life and is just returning to her people?" One might have thought still that the two may never see Naomi again and that they had done nothing wrong but freed themselves from barrenness, among other things. It certainly would have been in Ruth and Orpah's thoughts that they could now leave and possibly have children of their own elsewhere. It was that Orpah, the other wife, went her way. She had no sons for Naomi's other son, and she didn't seem to feel guilty for leaving the old woman.

But hidden in Ruth's name (which means "friend," "friendship," or "compassionate friend" [https://www.verywellfamily.com/ruth-name-meaning-origin-popularity-5211598#:~]) is love and the ability to take care of Naomi. Her decision to go with her mother-in-law was backed by an incredibly compassionate, loving, and powerful

God that wasn't hers but was borrowed from her Jewish mother-in-law. God certainly, and Naomi, would reward her mightily. God would ensure Ruth was cared for and positioned for greatness.

The holy scriptures do not tell us whether Ruth and Orpah were good women or wives. We are still not told how they handled barrenness during their ten years of marriage to Naomi's sons, what sadness may have accompanied the lives of these two Moabite women who were married to ill-fated brothers from Epthrathites.

Our willingness to please others before ourselves, among other reasons, could come from our love for God we have come to know and honor. Yet in a moment of life-changing decision, their true selves laid bare for all to see and to learn from, Ruth chose to go with and take care of her aging mother-in-law, and Orpah found it best to return to her own people.

The one thing we know of Ruth is that she was married to an Ephrathite, a Jew. But foreshadowing her meeting with her husband and Naomi, her soon-to-be ex-mother-in-law, was the impending birth of a son, Obed. Her marriage to Naomi's son was expected to produce sons to carry the lineage of Elimelek, the Ephrathites from Bethlehem and Judah, and not to end prematurely and without an heir.

Though not yet available to Ruth and Naomi, Obed would help change our journey of faith. Ruth would marry Naomi's son but would not have Obed with him; Obed's father would be a man still among her late husband's family, to be had only if she accompanied her mother-in-law back to her people. Choosing to go with Naomi, her mother-in-law, was exactly what she did. We know life has a way of starting with us, then turning us around, perhaps to bring us into the same loving place. God alone chooses where He births His babies.

According to the Bump, the name "Obed" means "servant of God, a worshipper" (https://www.thebump.com/b/obed-baby-name). Our Master Holy Spirit revealed to me that Ephrathites were worshippers of God.

Naomi and her family went to Egypt because of famine, leaving behind all they knew. According to Wikipedia, the word "Ephrath" means "fruitful," and according to Brittanica.com, "Bethlehem" means "house of bread" (https://en.wikipedia.org/wiki/Ephrath; https:// HYPERLINK "http://www.britannica.com/place/Bethlehem)" www.britannica.com/place/Bethlehem).

Humans may not see the glory of God in His plan for them in the immediate future, as it may seem laced with a covering of sorrow and sadness. But it will be divine in the end—pleasing, as it were, to body, souls, and spirits.

Death happens to all, rich and poor alike, and no partiality exists with death. We no longer have one thousand years available to us anymore, for humankind destroyed longer lifespans with his desires of the flesh. Now humans die sooner to lessen the pain and suffering the Old Serpent inflicted upon them. God prevents humans from worsening the darkness in this world by lowering their lifespans to seventy years or more (Psalm 90).

Naomi going back to Bethlehem was her retuning to the God of her people, the bread of life, the place of her salvation. Her home country of Bethlehem, house of bread, had become a wilderness of suffering, prompting an escape to Egypt. But we need more than bread to sustain truly meaningful lives. Our Lord Jesus Christ reminds us that people do not live by bread alone.

If we gain the whole world and acquire earthly riches, it profits us nothing, and we will not reach heaven if that's all we can show for our time here on earth. We will take none of our riches to eternity with us, as others will enjoy the work of our labor without a thought to the sufferings the benefactor incurred while acquiring them. We know that Hades is an awful place to spend eternity, particularly when we have already spent the few years His grace affords us on earth in opulence. These few years of prosperity cannot compare with the number of years called eternity. When we enjoy earthly riches, with God at the center of them, wow! We are to give generously, with clean hearts, to the needy among us, compassionately care for society's vulnerable ones, and do much more.

Most of us come to God when something bad happens. Otherwise, we go about enjoying our children, marriages, jobs, beautiful homes, cars, boats, creative works, relationships, and what have you, doing the things we do without a thought about the One Who made it all possible.

Let's go back to fully understand the emerging, yet unseen, Boaz–Ruth story. The Promised Seed was to come through Abraham's descendants, Isaac and Jacob (later renamed Israel by God after a divine encounter between God and Jacob). The blessed name changed Jacob, elevating him and all who were born to him. He will become the father of the twelve tribes of Israel.

Moabites are Lot's generations, born with his daughter after the fire of God destroyed Sodom and Gomorrah. Lot and his two daughters sought refuge inside a cave near the mountain area of

Zoar. In a way, Abraham raised Lot, for he took his brother's son with him when he responded to the call of God to leave his family to a land that He, God, would show Abraham.

An altercation between Abraham and Lot's servants, whose wealth in sheep and servants had grown exponentially, led to a separation between the two. Abraham asked Lot to choose a land in any direction and to possess the land of his chosen. Lot chose the seemingly great land of Sodom and Gomorrah and left Abraham for a new life with his family, servants, animals, and all his possessions.

Some people can be a hindrance to the plan of God in one's life. God's covenant relationship with Abraham began soon after. It would seem heaven was closed to Abraham before then, for he had embarked on the "home in the sky" journey God had asked him to embark on not alone but with his tagalong nephew. Not long after Lot let him, God began earnestly to lead Abram, whom He would later rename Abraham.

Lot's children would not mix with Abraham's descendants, for though related, their backgrounds made for contentious relationships between the two people. Israel was the people God had chosen for Himself. They had left the land of their forefather, Abraham, and were now in exile in Egypt.

They would not return to the Land God had promised Abraham's descendants for another 430 years. The Moabites worshipped Baal of Peor, and as Israel were on their way to the Promised Land, it was Lot's Moabites and Ammonites (sons by his other daughter) who hired Balaam to curse Israel.

God, loving Israel, would not honor such a curse, but these two people found a way to cause Israel to sin against God, raising God's anger against Israel. They had gotten Israel to lay with Moabite women (unauthorized women), which became a curse to Israel (Numbers 25).

Israel chose to serve more of other people's gods, being whimsical about the God of Abraham, the God of Isaac, and the God of Jacob. In this way, they billed other gods to be higher than their God. Boaz marrying Ruth is viewed as Boaz marrying an unauthorized woman, but God seemingly is involved in it.

Jacob gained property without authorization as well. He had cheated his brother Esau out of his blessings, then he had run away. But the Old Serpent was awaiting his opportunity to strike him. But God was watching.

Unauthorized grain causes our authorized blessings to be courageously switched. At the time of his marriage, Jacob's loving wife of his heart, Rachel, was switched, and Rachel's older sister Leah, in the cloak of the night, became Jacob's wife.

It would take Jacob fourteen years of hard labor to get what the Old Serpent had interfered with. Nonetheless, out of the unauthorized Jacob–Leah union came most of the tribes of Israel and only two from the loving authorized woman Rachel. Surprisingly, our Lord Jesus Christ would come from the unauthorized pairing of Jacob and Leah, Judah—a divine thought for you and me.

The unauthorized pair of Ruth and Boaz were now coupled as the result of a string of divinely unpredictable events. Let's recap! Naomi's husband, fleeing from famine, took his family to the land of grain, Moab. There she lost her husband and two sons, forcing her return to Bethlehem of Judea. Her womb now barren, she went home to God heirless. Arriving home alone, and barren, because her children barren in Egypt could not give their wives children, she was forced to devise a blessed plan to get her relatively young daughter-in-law to settle in her own home. Unbeknownst to both women, God was in the center of their loving plan.

Israel and Moab once more were about to perpetuate a pattern that had long existed before Naomi's daughter-in-law, Ruth, chose to return with her to blessed Bethlehem where she met Boaz, a member of her husband's clan. The combination of the chosen and the unauthorized was made to restore the relationship between God and His people. The seed of Boaz and Ruth will begin the return of Israel of God to worship, jointly lifting the name of the God of their forefathers.

Naomi helped Ruth obtain work on Boaz's large farm. In the kindness of his heart, he asked the other laborers to allow Ruth to harvest leftover grains (the leftover glory of God) for her mother-in-law, Naomi (who was made barren by the curses of the Old Serpent).

Ruth's reputation of selfless love and kindness toward her mother-in-law, Naomi, was in full display by now. Boaz was drawn into the nest of the divinely seductive Ruth and the mother-in-law's wisdom she heeded, and Ruth, well-positioned and prepared to capture the eye of older Boaz, lured him in. Boaz was pleased he had been chosen, especially by the younger Ruth. He bowed to the anointing of the young woman and grew immediately fond of her.

Ruth, now in good standing with Boaz, him being boldly positioned as the loving prince of God's people, was granted access to

Ruth's heart. Ruth had been married to a member of Boaz's clan. In reverence to the God of his people, Boaz followed the foundation of redeeming of the wife of a dead clan member. He offered her up to anyone who would want to marry her and buy the land Naomi's husband had left her as well.

Boaz believed in the kindness within his own lineage. His great-grandfather was Amminadab whose name means "my people (or my kinsman) is generous or noble" (https://www.biblestudytools.com/dictionary/amminadab/). Abarim's translation takes it a little further "People of Liberality, My Kinsman Is Noble," adding, "From (1) the noun עם ('am), kinsman or people, and (2) the verb nadab), to willingly give" (https://www.abarim-publications(נדב)com/Meaning/Amminadab.html). It would seem this noble family were "kinsman redeemers." He was here now to redeem Ruth (looming in the future, Lord Jesus Christ would come to redeem the Gentiles as well).

Grain-providing Boaz begins laying the foundation on which our Lord Jesus Christ, the bread of life, redeemer, and King would be born. By his kindness toward Ruth of Naomi, Boaz secured the blessings of grain of life (our Lord Jesus Christ).

Peculiar in Boaz's lineage are the names his father and grandfather are given, which begin to link us liberally to the Garden of Eden, among other things.

Selfless Boaz, wanting to do what was right, trusted God to honor Himself and waited his turn in the family line to marry Ruth. Boaz received the blessings from his kin and succeeded in marrying beloved Ruth. In doing so, he solved a mystery.

Boaz's father was Salmon. As we trace Lord Jesus Christ's lineage, we see that Boaz is of His ancestry, making Boaz's father, Salmon, an ancestor of David, thus of our Lord Jesus Christ.

The name "Salmon" derives from the "Hebrew word shalom/shelomoh, meaning peace, completeness (in number), safety, soundness (in body), welfare, health, prosperity, quiet, tranquility, contentment, friendship, or human relationships [—] with God especially in covenant relationship" (https://www.name-doctor.com/name-salmon-meaning-of-salmon-47755.html).

The meaning of "Salmon"—which includes "peace . . . friendship, or human relationships, with God especially in covenant relationship"—is evident in the way Boaz's father's name connects with Lord Jesus Christ. In the full meaning of his name is the awareness that people were expected to live safe, contented, quiet, tranquil, and prosperous lives, which speaks of welfare under the glorious shadow of God.

Salmon's name joins us to the covenant relationship humanity has with God. Salmon's father was Nahshon, the son of Amminadab of Judah. Nahshon's sister, was Elisheba, or "Eli and Sheva" ("Eli [—] 'My God' and 'the number with the holy attributes: 'seven'"). The name then means "My God of the Seventh"; "Sheva" may also mean "swear." The meaning of the name, then, is "(In) My God (I) swear" (https://hebrew.jerusalemprayerteam.org/elisheba-elizabeth-elisabeth-2/). She was the wife of Aaron, the elder brother of Moses, letting us know Boaz's family was close to the liberation of Jews, God's chosen children.

Salmon's father, Nahshon, was a member of the army, and his name means "serpent" (https:// HYPERLINK "http://www.

abarim-publications.com/" www.abarim-publications.com/Meaning/Nahshon.html). Numbers 1:7, 2:3 shows that Nahshon, son of Amminadab, was selected by Moses and Aaron by the command of Almighty God, to represent Judah, his tribe.

The Master Holy Spirit said Nahshon was wise, cunning, deceptive, and dependable in his fighting skills against his enemies. The Old Serpent too was skilled (in work, through the snake, and in spirit, as Satan) in seeking to dethrone Adam through Eve; but good always overcomes evil, and Adam's generations were divinely positioned for victory.

Follow us kindly as our Master Holy Spirit shows us how wonderfully connected what happened to Ruth, Naomi, and Boaz is to the Garden of Eden and to our Lord Jesus Christ's work of salvation.

Two brothers minimally show us what was to come (flesh, giving glory to Satan; light of life, glorifying God). Genesis 4 introduces Cain and Abel. By his name's meaning being "serpent," it is clear that Boaz's grandpa, Nahshon, belonged to the line of Gentiles (sinful flesh, Cain), but he was boldly transformed in his son Salmon (Abel), Boaz's father. By his name "Salmon," the family moved from the name and mannerism of the Old Serpent to one named and having the mannerism of the prince of peace. Our Lord Jesus Christ would be called the Prince of Peace.

Cain worked the soil. He brought an offering of fruit to God. Beloved God saw the deception in Cain and rejected his offering; he withheld the good of the land from God, an evil act. Abel, his younger brother, kept flocks (unifying God's children). He was in the similitude of the good shepherd (Lord Jesus Christ). He was willing to give to God what belonged to God, his honored flocks. So

Abel offered God his best and the greatest of his quality flocks (from the "bottom of his heart"), and God gloriously accepted it.

Cain became angry, bowing his face to the ground. Cain (unstable earth), experienced shame, rejection, anger, wickedness, greed, small in his own eyes, and fear of not being good enough, and he launched a counterattack on his brother. Cain, lost firmly in his own bold desires, and in a jealous rage, killed his brother Abel. Cain had taken on the personality of the Old Serpent.

Satan, seeing how God loved Adam, in a fit of greed, selfishness, anger, and evil to the core, entered the serpent. He became the Old Serpent, used Eve, and, in a bold deceptive move, got God's servant, Adam, killed, physically and spiritually, and removed Adam from the glorious presence of God. In the order of the Old Serpent, Cain had disobeyed God and destroyed he who was good, Abel.

Ensuing practices of humans grounded either in good spirit (light and goodness) or in greedy flesh (the wickedness of and the evil in humankind) were found in these two brothers, who were born after Adam and Eve were driven out from the Garden of Eden.

Blessings and curses can skip a generation, and so "curses" of Nahshon did not settle in Salmon, his son. Salmon transformed boldly into a completely different person, not the "snake" his father was known to have been.

Rahab, loved by God, received the blessing of marriage and outwitted the Old Serpent (Nahshon), married him, and lovingly birthed Salmon. Rahab's grandson Boaz, son of Salmon, continued lovingly moving humankind toward the coming birth of our Lord Jesus Christ.

The good-heartedness and thoughtfulness that operated in Boaz seemed to be rooted in his father's, Salmon's, love of God and in his upbringing, as evident in the name of his grandpa, Amminadab ("kinsman redeemer").

Obed, the child born to Ruth and Boaz by divine connection, brings Israel back to God. With the grace for the worship of God in spirit and in truth greatly secured, Obed gives birth to Jesse (Yishai).

The Hebrew name "Yishai," which means "the Lord exists" (https:// HYPERLINK "http://www.thebump.com/b/yishai-baby-name)" www.thebump.com/b/yishai-baby-name), is the name "Jesse," "which either means 'God exists,' or 'King'" (https://en.wikipedia.org/wiki/Jesse(given name)), and was given to Boaz and Ruth's grandson, the father of God's anointed, David, a bold worshipper of God.

The patriarch Abraham saw the vision of the Lamb of God, who would be slain for humankind, as he obeyed God's call for him to take his promised son, Isaac, and sacrifice him to God on Mount Moriah. Prophetically too, David saw the crucifixion of Lord Jesus Christ, the Messiah, who would fulfill God's promise of a Seed that would bruise the head of the Old Serpent, securing humankind's salvation. His visions are laced excellently across the book of Psalms.

In her sacrificial giving of self, believing in the God of her mother-in-law Naomi, Ruth returned humankind back to God.

Our Lord Jesus is given a name above every other name. Ruth was graciously brought into the lineage that brought us David—a man after God's own heart, the great worshipper, the giant slayer, the great King of Israel, one who taught us to make our boast in the

Lord, a Psalmist who reminds us of varied strategies for defeating the devil. He did so, too, through the many ways he served God. Ruth showed us what the righteous ones ought to do when their foundations are destroyed; they are to chase after God boldly and lovingly.

We should take a page from gracious Ruth's book to expand our territory through giving fully of ourselves without negotiating with Satan in any way; it would bring us before God.

We are too quick to look for what we can get from others before we can help them or give away anything. We do the same with God, our Father. God looks for what to give us, His precious daughters, regardless of who or what we are.

Women like Hannah and Ruth, wounded of God, hold mysteries of great import to humanity. We can see that these women experienced many pitfalls but rose above them. The secret of their successes was that they believed God, trusted God, were selfless for God, worked for God, desired God, made sacrifices for God, and loved God.

Women ought to make a joyful noise for God's perfect timing, grace, location, and loving positioning for their lives. When things are not working out or don't work out, we are not to panic; there just might be God's hands at work in that situation.

These women centered their lives on God, giving God their best, and went the extra mile to make sure their lives were pleasing to God and their fellow humans. It is good to know that Hannah's son, the prophet Samuel, anointed God's chosen David, great-grandson of Ruth, as the king of Israel many years before he even became king.

CHAPTER 7

Anointed Esther: Guided by the God of Impossibilities

We know the blessing of the wise goes a long way in the lives of those who possess Esther's wisdom. How does an uncle, a palace gateman, except by divine intervention, get the wisdom to ask his cousin, an unqualified orphan, a young girl in his care, to participate in the greatest beauty pageant ever held to gain a queen for the king?

At the gate, you get to hear conversations from both the commoners who pass by the palace to see whether they can catch a glimpse of the royals and the princes who visit the palace but stop at the gate to gain inside knowledge of the happenings inside the palace before going in to meet the king. The gate is a place of light exchanges and a place where lives can be reshaped. It also can be a place of access to information that can elevate or demote any life.

There was something peculiar about the chain of events that took place to set the stage for a very simple gatekeeper, Mordecai, to emerge as the wisdom of the old and an orphan girl (Hadassah, Esther) as a heroine for us women and for her beloved nation.

King Ahasuerus was to give a party in the third year of his reign, and the decision agreed with God's imminent plan for the Jews, for God knew what lay ahead. God is the one who can raise up one king and bring down another.

We are privileged to review the life of young Hadassah who, guided by her uncle, was elevated to become one of the mothers of change for Israel.

Hadassah's uncle was a man who knew the times and seasons of God for the nation of Israel, even in exile. Mordecai was aware of God's love for Israel and had privileged knowledge of her enemies in the provinces. Mordecai feared God and would not bow to the enemies of God.

Mordecai had received information about the need for the palace to get all the beautiful women from the citadel and its more than 127 provinces to participate in a kingly beauty pageant. The pageant would produce a queen to replace the dethroned Queen Vashti.

God had devised a plan to help silence Israel's foe and the avenger (the Old Serpent). Perhaps, should Israel not survive in exile, the Messiah, Savior of mankind (Lord Jesus Christ) promised to Adam and Eve in the Garden of Eden, would be late in coming. The Promised Seed that God said would bruise the head of the Old Serpent was still looming.

Vashti's fall from grace would have been a subject of common discussions among ideal minds and nothing more. The eventual gatekeeper, Mordecai, however, saw the hand of God in the moment. The search for a new queen was no longer a causal discussion but a momentous one, and it would impact many lives. The gatekeeper hatched a divinely led plan to bring down the hand of God.

It is possible that Hadassah would have married a nice boy and had a good life, oblivious to what was being hatched by Haman, the enemy of the Jews. Mordecai, understanding the times and season, gave a new narrative to the beauty pageant.

Mordecai recommended his cousin Hadassah participate in the beauty pageant. Though herself beautiful, winning the pageant on her own merit would have been impossible; for starters, she was unqualified, as a Jew. Each woman in the pageant had to complete a prescribed beauty treatment of six months with oil of myrrh (symbolically, so she would die to the flesh) and six months of perfumes and cosmetics treatment (to attract God's King's attention).

Hadassah (Esther) won the pageant and became queen, having found favor with God, who prepared Hadassah to win the favors of Hegai, who oversaw the harem and was divinely positioned to assist her and the king, who chose an illegal participant for his queen.

Vashti's unforced error, dishonoring her husband, the king, had changed the nature of power at the citadel. Esther, now queen, with the help of her cousin Mordecai, would determine the faith of Jews in the citadel and the provinces. Mordecai also had heard about a plot to kill the king and communicated this to Queen Esther who shared the information with the king, foiling the enemies' murderous plot.

A plan from God to rescue His wonderfully and fearfully made people was beginning to take shape. But an enemy yet in the shadow named Haman would formulate a plan to annihilate the Jews in the provinces stretching from India to Cush (Ethiopia).

Among those in the citadel and the provinces might also have been those of the lineage of the Promised Seed, our Lord Jesus Christ, the root of Jesse. The Old Serpent's instigated plan to kill all Jews, if successful, could change God's plan, leading our Lord Jesus Christ to be born somewhere else. Queen Esther headed the plan to rescue the Jews, her beloved people.

In the tapestry of this story is the wisdom of our great God. God had found two great messengers, Queen Esther and Mordecai, to ensure the protection of the foundation of our Lord Jesus Christ.

God, Father of our Lord Jesus Christ, exposed the seriousness of what was to come for mankind in the similitude of the magi coming from the east, opening their treasure chests, and presenting baby Jesus with gold, frankincense, and myrrh. The similitude was laid bare in the palace garden. The gift of gold referenced the Kingship of our Lord Jesus Christ: Frankincense spoke to the surrealness, suffering, and pain that awaited Him and Myrrh spoke of the mortification of the immortal man (lowly risen King).

At the palace at the citadel of Susa, some mysteries were embedded in the layout of its garden. To an ordinary eye, it was a well-laid-out display of beauty and splendor. The mundane things around us often hold mysteries that we must at times decode to fully understand how they impact our lives and to benefit from them. Let's follow our Master Holy Spirit to see what was hidden in plain sight.

God had given Queen Esther multiple graces to overcome the wickedness of Haman, though this was unknown to her and her people.

"⁵And when these days were expired, the king made a feast unto all the people that were present in Shushan the palace, both unto great and small, seven days, in the court of the garden of the king's palace; ⁶Where were white, green, and blue, hangings, fastened with cords of fine linen and purple to silver rings and pillars of marble: the beds were of gold and silver, upon a pavement of red, and blue, and white, and black, marble" (Esther 1:5–6).

Unbeknownst to the people, the diabolical plan of Haman had beneath them the wisdom (and graces) that God would give Esther while she was yet a participant in the beauty pageant and as Queen, In His Holy Word, God always promises He would go before His children to straighten the crooked places.

Unobtrusive, but hidden in the garden display, were symbols of the destruction of the Jews that would soon be apparent. But the Creator of the heavens and the earth had also mapped out a plan to destroy the source of the problem; these too were embedded in the garden design.

Let's now decode the garden's loving designs. The white, green, and blue mix fastened with cords of fine linen meant gifts associated with each of the three colors were joined together with an understanding of who God is, giving Hadassah, yet in the pageant, a winning beauty, serious graces for subduing her enemies (as contestant and as Queen) and a wonderful awareness of the awesomeness of

God. She had no knowledge of the many other gifts that she would need that God had already stored in her.

As Queen Esther, she was given divine courage, strength, self-sacrifice, vulnerability that would turn around the strong to a weakened foe (Haman). These gifts were placed inside her to help her control the attention and focus of the King and to strengthen her; she would need more than her gracious beauty to sustain her and save her people. This would unfold in the coming together of her beloved people in a heart unified in both purpose and a show of their loving ties to God.

The garden design of white hid an earthly cloud of witnesses (and the blessings of the Master Holy Spirit). The green in the design gave glorification to God and blessings to all who would effectively assist Queen Esther. The blue, kingship, alerted Hadassah to the fight that was ahead. In heaven, our Lord Jesus Christ who was to come (Man of sorrow, royalty, sacrificial Lamb) was evident in the blue. The mix of these three colors (white, green, and blue) would bless her greatly as Hadassah and as the Queen. The Savior's grace was therefore placed in the garden for her, as good and evil would soon collide and the Old Serpent's anger would be unleashed, joining with Haman. The Holy Spirit was there to help her triumph.

These hangings were fastened to cords of fine linen (goodness), letting us know the mind of the renewed Queen to save her people, and to purple to silver rings (suffering and death), in the similitude of the death of the innocent one with ties to heaven and earth (our Lord Jesus Christ). However, in what was to happen in the palace (a foreshadowing of what was to come for mankind), these designs signified the fact that in the not-so-distant future there would be the pain of a royal one who, in agony, would not hesitate to die for the betterment of her people.

As the plot to destroy all Jews unfolded, Queen Esther declared a national fast to strengthen her in the honor of God and to fulfill her assignment. Surprisingly, her people did not show any pride, arrogance, or judgment; nor did they argue when asked, but they cooperated from an inner knowing of God's voice.

The Master Holy Spirit said that there were designs in the Garden of Eden that had been placed lovingly to capture the courageous salvation of mankind.

The gatekeeper, Mordecai, stirred Haman's anger because he would not bow to him, the second in command in the palace. We too are asked not to bow to earthly wealth, because it would make us momentarily comfortable.

When the crown of God's love is over a person or people, though it may not be noticeable to the naked eye, we cannot tamper with them; doing so would be touching God's winning heart. There are repercussions for harming those God considers the apple of His eyes, including you and me. It may have been better that Haman limited his anger to brining Mordecai to death for his dishonoring behavior, for Mordecai would not bow to Haman when he would pass by him at the gate. But Haman extended the plan to kill to include all the Jews in the citadel and the more than 127 provinces.

Esther's saving of the Jews is a warning to all who seek to destroy the innocent. God's covering over Israel remains our covering, for we are the spiritual children of Abraham.

The queen had no children of her own, but in a glorious amazement, this barren woman would now be a mother of the nation she would lead to safety, to the disgrace of the foe and avenger (the Old Serpent in the person of Haman).

Our attention is now drawn to the purple to silver rings and pillars of marble in the garden design, on which the white, green, and blue hangings were fastened on cords of fine linen. This spoke to the upcoming destruction of the wealth, opulence, and peaceful lifestyle the Jews in the citadel and across the more than 127 provinces had acquired. God would showcase Himself once again. He who saved Israel came with them through the wilderness where serpents and scorpions abounded. Once again, they would be going through another wilderness of unprovoked, demeaning attacks.

Hidden, then, in plain sight in this garden design was a show of disdain, hatred, and open jealousy toward a people whose hard work had provoked the anger of an old enemy. The Old Serpent knew that from this bloodline would come the Promised Seed, and he would seek to use Haman to annihilate them.

It is only fitting then that Queen Esther was the secret built into the complex display in the palace garden. Additionally, "the beds were of gold and silver, upon a pavement of red, and blue, and white, and black, marble."

Let's examine these. The "beds" spoke of rest from the grievous attack by one who would use money he had accumulated—gold (wealth) and silver (suffering)—to annihilate the Jews. These were upon a pavement of red (i.e., blood) and blue (i.e., courageous king) and white (i.e., beautiful savior), and black (i.e., death) marble (of the lies of the wealthy, powerful supporters of Haman). This woman of strength, Queen Esther, her guardian Mordecai, and the blessed people of God, the Jews, would all join to give Haman a resounding defeat.

Out of Haman flowed the Old Serpent's plan to control the palace lines of authority, and in a show of wealth, he offered the king money in exchange for the power to destroy the Jews, but the king wanted no part of it. Haman would violate existing rules, writing new ones that usurped the powers of the king, preventing the king duly from protecting the Jews.

The bold combined power of the Jews, in obedience to God, fasting to lower the power of the Old Serpent, evolved as a momentous weapon of love—something the Old Serpent could not stop. Queen Esther emerged as a courageous protector of the Jew. A union of husband and wife, two working together, is a powerful weapon against the onslaught of Satan, the Old Serpent. Queen Esther, with the support of her husband, savior of her people, collided with those who had the power to destroy the Jews.

The unusual powers that God had hidden in Esther, symbolic in the garden designs, would now work in her favor to bring her people together for victory. Queen Esther arose to save her people, wrestling them out of the clutches of the Old Serpent, evil Haman.

The power of Haman over the palace and its more than 127 provinces from India to Cush collided with Queen Esther, resulting in the deaths of major pillars of power, including Haman, Haman's ten sons, their families, and the politicians who cleverly secured Haman's evil plots to annihilate all Jews.

Queen Esther was about to demonstrate the great wisdom, formidable strength, savior grace, divine beauty, knowledge, understanding, and bold morality bestowed upon her by God. God Almighty can bring forth gifts given to His children in private, only to showcase them in public through events that unfold.

In acknowledgment of the completion of the temple Solomon's father, David, couldn't build for God but helped put together what would be needed to ensure its completion, the scriptures tell us God blessed King Solomon with wisdom after Solomon offered a thousand burnt offerings on the altar at Gibeon. God had visited Solomon in a night dream.

God asked Solomon what he wanted, as He was satisfied with Solomon's offering. He asked for a discerning heart to govern God's people and the ability to distinguish between right and wrong. God honored Solomon with a discerning heart, wisdom, riches, world-renowned fame, and the inspiration to write the books of Ecclesiastes and Proverbs and the Song of Solomon.

In the fullness of time, a secret situation arose causing God to showcase publicly what he had given Solomon in a dream through a mysterious set of unfolding events.

One morning, two harlots (1 Kings 3:16–28) who shared the same house came to King Solomon, asking him to settle an issue they had. One had lain on her three-day-old baby in the night, killing the infant. Unbeknownst to these women, heaven was watching.

The Old Serpent, in the person of the woman with the dead baby, proceeded to switch her dead child with the living baby belonging to her friend. The Old Serpent failed to know that women's wombs are equipped with divine vision.

It was not him who had died in the covering of the night; that was a lie. The case brought to King Solomon would showcase the gift of wisdom God had given him. He asked for a sword to split the living baby in half. The woman with the dead child, wanting neither of them to have a living child, asked the king to go ahead and divide the living baby—greed, disobedience, and wickedness, the Old Serpent's strategies.

We easily give away gifts God has given us. Israel had turned away from God. They were worshipping other gods. The mother hoped that, when the infant grew up, he would find her (Israel's return to her God, I daresay).

God, guided by love for His people, as in this mother's plea (she called out to the king to give the child to her lying friend), gave back to the Jews their wealth and life of opulence. King Solomon judged in favor of the godly mother, giving her the child, letting the Old Serpent know that the God of Israel judges still.

When Israel heard about the verdict, they held the king in awe, knowing then that the gift of divine wisdom was upon him and he was going to judge Israel lovingly and with justice.

The world was about to see the gifts God deposited in Hadassah, the soon-to-be Queen Esther. Daniel 2:21 lets us know God changes the times and seasons. He deposes one king and raises another.

There are "Esthers" even in our own families: great-grandmothers who save their families from brokenness by giving them insights on family foundation problems, thereby preventing the wreckage of future generations. In our loving nature (wombs), we carry divine mysteries. Women are victoriously called to grow winning wombs to cancel the plantings of deceivers in our gardens. Our Esthers, therefore, are women who put everything on the line, risking their queenships to save their people, even their families.

These wonderful displays of power by our truly anointed Queen Esther (Hadassah) to subdue evil totally are evident in the hearts of many of today's women.

Queen Esther gained access to heavenly love, honor, glory, control of secrets in the palace, blessings of God, and mind-bending strength by fasting with her people. These glorious gifts subdued the king. It made it difficult for him to focus on anything but her, helping to fulfill the glorious tasks of saving the Jews.

Queen Esther appeared before her husband, the king, unauthorized—an unheard-of act worthy of death. She survived dethronement for her blatant disregard of the king's authority because God was with her; He changed protocols for her sake. The king stretched out his scepter of loving appreciation, making the coming salvation of her people possible instead. Who can fathom the depth of our God's mighty power and authority?

Our Esther did not perish then because she had God's backing and had gotten the marble in the garden to bow. The Old Serpent in the person of Haman bowed before God's marble, Queen Esther. God's covering over Queen Esther, the chosen one, unleashed a seemingly overly glorious and unquenchable deliverance of greatness, bearing down the power of heaven on her.

The life of Ruth who cunningly lived in the shadow is seen in that of Esther. A loving and guided courtship authorized to win Boaz's heart was equally bad, but both women were divinely positioned to move Israel toward God. Truly, these women who worked lovingly in cooperation with God laid solid foundations for the women to come after them.

Among other things, Queen Esther held two successfully orchestrated banquets, calling only the king and her nemesis, to reveal the wickedness of this old rival Haman who wished to annihilate the Jews. Built for the deliverance of her people, Queen Esther gave a second dinner, calling again only the king and Haman. It was here that she revealed her identity (illegal and unqualified as she was) to her husband, the king, as well as the true purpose of the invitation. (Gone are the days when we would call everyone to release the happenings in our lives.)

We should trust and serve God to minimize the havoc the Old Serpent can wreak in many areas of our lives, releasing details of our lives only when we have too. One good man of God, Apostle Joshua Selman, noted that truth is sequential; I am paraphrasing. Outside of its proper context, truth being told for truth's sake may not make sense or may cause much harm.

King Ahasuerus allowed Queen Esther and Mordecai to victoriously, graciously, and immediately write new decrees to overrule and override Haman's decrees to destroy all Jews in the citadel and across the more than 127 provinces.

The Old Serpent lurks still in every area of life: families, relationships, jobs, ministries, churches, communities, institutions, and the larger society. The Old Serpent can enter a family and destroy them using the people they allow into their lives. Sometimes these infiltrators are wrong spouses who, enveloped in evil, can divide the families they are married into. These wicked people can divide people into warring camps, causing unbearable pain, and solving these problems can take some time. These also can be conniving friends, killer coworkers, fallen men or women of God, cunning neighbors, and those who teach evil and prejudices to children.

Queen Esther and her people's victory is our victory, and today we stand to acknowledge the sovereignty and supremacy of God over the unseen, the seen, and all of eternity.

Our blessed Queen Esther will forever remind us that one person can change situations and circumstances. So we are to be the Esther we are lovingly, even in the challenging situations impacting our lives, families, careers, churches, communities, institutions, and more. We are to overtake and blot out evil handwritings with the blood of Jesus, overrule any evil decrees and actions, change policies, develop greater reliance on God, nail ordinances to the cross, and boldly attack ungodly foes, regardless of how they present.

Unqualified to participate in the greatest pageant to find a queen for the king, this frightened and seemingly ill-equipped young woman stood in the gap for a nation. Backed by heaven, she and her people subdued the wicked plans of the Old Serpent, a very powerful enemy, Haman. God has divinely hidden a tapestry for our victory and greatness in the gardens of our lives and society. We are grateful!

CHAPTER 8

The Shunammite Woman: A Serious Worshipper of God

The Shunammite woman shows us the mighty destruction and humiliation of Satan's plans to override God's plans for our lives. This woman's unwavering belief in God calls our attention to the blessings we receive when we open our lives to entertain God.

Her case was brought before Prophet Elisha not long after he had solved a pressing problem in the home of a late prophet of God. Before we get to her, let's see what happened on the road that led to her place.

The prophet had just died, leaving his family in abject poverty and plagued by debtors. One of the debtors wanted to take the prophet's two sons as payment for the debt owed to him. The late prophet's wife approached Prophet Elisha to tell him about the creditor.

Elisha, upon hearing the problem and seeing her fears, asked the woman whether she had anything he could use to bless her to enable repayment of her debts. She told him she had only a small jar of oil left at home. Lost in grief, she saw the oil jar as small, causing the Old Serpent to rejoice over her lack of divine perception.

The unmatched blessings of God in our lives can come in small jars. The Old Serpent tells us lies that can cause us to minimize what we have or who we are, for his own purpose. Knowing God can expand a small jar of oil, the prophet asked her to borrow many empty vessels from her neighbors; she asked her sons to get the vessels. When they arrived with the blessed vessels, she shut the door behind (leave logic, earthly realities, and earthly thoughts) them and pour the oil into the borrowed empty containers. She did as the prophet had instructed, and the small jar of oil did not stop flowing into the borrowed vessels until she ran out of vessels (2 Kings 4:1–7). May the wildernesses in our lives become fruitful vines and our fruitful vines plenty of forests. The flow of oils in our lives (the presence of our Master Holy Spirit) offers us great possibilities. She went back to the prophet who then told her to go and sell the oil, pay her debts, and live off her profits.

The old graces of sowing seeds of goodness secured her future. God had released into their lives resources to help change their dire situation, saving them from the pitfalls of poverty. The great reward of work done for God by the dead prophet had been his family's saving grace (honor, favor, and victory), which changed the sorrow in their lives to joy.

Prophet Elisha was on his way to another town when he encountered the wife of the late prophet, and the miracle of overwhelming expansion followed. (A small jar of oil turned into a river of resource that sustained a family.)

The path to God can contain stops that are either planned or unplanned. Even these stops have values that they bring into our lives' journeys.

Things happen in our lives and may often look like true disasters, and we would like God to please move them away from us. These seeming disasters too have benefits if we keep our eyes on the larger picture of God's purpose for our lives, knowing that our lives are connected to those of others, either for good or bad. I feel like crying at times, for life seemingly has not turned out the way I had envisioned. I am learning that the evolution of newness that is Christ in me, the Hope of Glory, brings both joy and eternal peace even during thundering storms.

I am learning still to turn my gaze from my selfish desires (those that do not serve our Heavenly Father's needs) to a broader assessment of life, the big picture, and appreciate all the great wonders Jesus Christ, our Lord, who gave all for me, is doing in my little life and in the wider world.

But as I sit with the Holy Spirit, our Master, gaining divine wisdom (Psalm 113), I feel exceedingly blessed by the potholes, bumps, hiccups, sorrow, and good grinds on the path of life; I would not change anything.

Many of us today are reaping the blessings our parents left behind. Their good works are remembered by our God who loved us and never forgets our labor of love—a connection to our Master Holy Spirit! The woman with the flowing jar of endless oil was a beneficiary of her husband's blessed labor of love for a God who connects us all to the source of all power.

Elisha headed to the town of Shunem, whose name means "their change" (https:// HYPERLINK "http://www.sheknows.com/baby-names/name/" www.sheknows.com/baby-names/name/shunem/#). There he was met by a woman who had provided food for him in the past. But something was different now. The woman had been observing Prophet Elisha's movement around town and now perceived him to be a prophet of God. The Shunammite woman shared her observations with her husband, deciding then to create a room in their home for him. She wanted Prophet Elisha to have a place to rest his head in her home whenever he would come to town. She prepared the room and offered it to him, and he accepted her gesture of kindness.

Our Lord Jesus Christ was on His way to heal the dying daughter of Jairus, an official at the local synagogue. But a joy was overshadowing a woman who for twelve years had been suffering from the issue of blood that endlessly poured out of her. One suffering from such a problem is one with no life left in oneself and can't work, play, dance, live life to the fullest, praise God, or fulfill one's God-given purpose in life. I know one such young woman. She was living with a constant menstrual flow that depleted her blood levels. The last time she went to the hospital, she was a marvel; doctors from various disciplines came to see her. Her blood level was so low she ought to have been dead, but God was with her. Healed, she was lovingly left to fulfill the purpose of God.

The woman with the issue of blood, believing that the Lord Jesus Christ was God from what she had heard behind the scenes, encouraged herself and gently approached the crowd around Him and pushed her way through. She proceeded to touch the hem of our Lord Jesus's healing garment, for He was a divine source for her and our deliverance.

Giving glory to God by her faith in the one true God in that moment, unbeknownst to her, she had touched Eternity (the blood of Jesus, which was to be shed for all on the Cross of Calvary, responded). In that moment, the Old Serpent in her blood, the uncontrollable outflowing of the lifeblood in her, fled. Evil that had consumed her life, her earnings, and her life's purpose stopped its onslaught instantly.

The Shunammite woman had provided the prophet a small peculiar room on the wall (roof) of her house that had in it only a bed, a table, a chair, and a lamp.

To judge this four-item room as being bare would be to miss the point. As in the case of Queen Esther, where the items in the garden laid bare a mystery, this setup offers mysterious insights into God's plans for this kind family. We know nothing goes past God, and we could see His hand at work here again.

I had visited a food court one day, during one of my shopping sprees at the mall. The Master asked me to circle a table of a woman and her two sons having lunch. I later asked our Master Holy Spirit why I had been asked to circle the family. I was told the food had been poorly constituted and prepared. His presence, released by the action I was instructed to take, had served as a source of divine intervention, allowing the family to enjoy a glorious meal instead. God's children never truly understand the ways by which our lives are saved.

Before we look at the spiritual meanings of these items in the room on the wall (at the top), it is important to point out a little scripture we miss (elevating the well) when we read this story.

We see first that it was the Shunammite woman who noticed the full movements of the man of God, perceiving him to be a prophet, and observed he needed a place to rest his head (the mind of God). We are reminded once more that women are key to mankind's yielding to God, willingly observing the hand of God in their kindred and salvation. She was the one who knew their visitor Elisha to be a holy man of God.

When she first met him, she urged him to eat bread at her house, creating a comfort zone; whenever he would come to town, he could eat there. This woman shared her insights about their dinner guest with her husband and quickly moved to creating a room for him. That's what our love for our God does to us. When you encounter God, you too won't be able to contain yourself; you will make room for Him in your life and family.

The Shunammite woman demonstrated a love for God and a mastery of womanhood in her actions: she saw, attacked, elevated, and conquered. Before long, the man of God had a lovely place in her home, as if God were resting there.

In many of our homes, there's room for a prophet, be it a spouse or child becoming more than we first observe or perceive him or her to be. Make room for such prophets at the top (mind), for the potential transformation that God can bring about in them at any time.

We women see things and tell ourselves we will get to them. Husbands see them and immediately say them, looking like the geniuses that they are (ha ha!). I am a very spoiled wife and am terribly guilty of that. Much of it is because we want peace to reign, ignoring our subtle important roles as women, trying not to cause arguments. But we create imbalances instead of the peace we seek, for the strategy to not voice things or speak up, for peace's sake, has never worked (grace and wisdom). There are many homes still where our husbands are so detached from everyday duties that it is we wives who must remind them of their daily family responsibilities.

At times, we are seen as the frailer gender, lacking in wisdom, having no intuition, and, worse yet, being not-so-good wives. Husbands don't understand we are cooperating with God, trying not to drive them away by being too mouthy. Yet we can't give up being loving, caring, strong, emboldened, confident, visionary, accommodating, and true to womanhood. We must still ask God to help us balance our lives, roles, and responsibilities while remaining wispier.

We are God's gifts to our men. The room was on the wall (at the rooftop, having the covering of God). The Shunammite woman was not sure Elisha was a prophet of God but perceived him to be one. She had been providing food for the perceived holy man, so we can safely say she was already eating with God. She had a qualified belief in God. You can't see the God we serve, then get to know Him by His doings in your life (although subtle) and the blessings you see in the lives of those around you.

The Shunammite woman was moving in her understanding of who God is, in a deeper realm of knowing. We are not to wait until we see God, or the hand of God, to acknowledge His sovereignty, supremacy, or existence. It is no accident that she had set the room where she had and provided for the man of God the specific items found therein. There were divine writings in both the items displayed in the room and in the location of the room.

Good befalls those who are in the council of the upright. Feeding a prophet of God, the Shunammite woman reaped a prophet's reward. The possible reward of knowing a prophet of God was not a priority, as she was already wealthy, influential, and seemed to have no inert need. But in making food available from a genuine place of love, the Shunammite woman invariably was feeding God. He would favor her labor of love and prosper the work of their hands later.

The room held a bed and a table among its four items. The table symbolizes the blessings of riches and the power of God over the works of their hands. The Shunammite woman and her husband ensured their riches was firmly preserved by giving the prophet the room on the wall (roof), signifying a higher-order relationship between them and God. The bed and table being together indicated they were going to have real wealth (i.e., joy, peace, gladness, favor, and riches).

The Shunammite woman understood how God had blessed them. The bed (mind at rest to gather riches) being connected to the table (gathering of wealth and opulence) was symbolic of a productive life.

These two items—a bed and a table, in any room in which one is seeking to find rest—truly envelop all that comfort brings. Through her kindness of giving the man of God a room in which to breathe after a day's work, God, who provides food for those who love Him, dredges up His covenant of fruitfulness for the woman.

Scripture reminds us that our belief in the power of God and the gifts He has given to His prophets are to prosper us believers. It was scriptural, then, how and where she placed the room and furniture. Our whole lives are spent before God who sits enthroned in heaven, seeing us, His children, from an elevated perspective, watering our lives.

The Shunammite woman cunningly well positioned the Prophet Elisha so he would be able to assess their lives more clearly from the top, giving him the opportunity to better help them.

There are secret needs that manifest when we come into the presence of a prophet of God. A major gift of a child in one's old age reflects a wonderful reversal of the awful cloak of barrenness Satan used to cover the life of this family. What was meant to humiliate this very wealthy couple places them now squarely in a position to showcase the wonder of God, His power, mercy, and love. Delay is not denial, and encountering God changes our situation.

We want to hear from God regardless of the level of success we have attained in life. This woman wanted the rested prophet to humiliate the enemies of God, for his voice hosted heaven.

The weeping in the night, caused by the Old Serpent, would now be heard by the man of God resting on the wall (at their roof), calming their minds.

Blessings of wealth and riches are incomplete when God is not glorified by them. God told Adam and Eve to go and multiply and be fruitful, to boldly be productive and complete each other. This family seemingly had been no "fruit-bearing tree" for God to water to produce the specific fruits (children) they needed in their lives.

Though loved by her rich husband, the Shunammite woman had not produced an heir like Hannah. Heaven was opened to her and her husband now.

There was also a chair in the room at the top. A chair usually denotes a settling in one's home, but hers was yet to be settled. A woman without a chair, if she desires one, lovingly may feel unhappy, though possessing great wealth.

Moreover, her husband was aging, and she too was advancing in age. By Divine direction and guidance, the prophet's feet had brought him into their family.

Their feet would walk a different path going forward. Prophet Elisha, a carrier of God's word, was on their roof, and this upward thinking meant their currently impossible situation (no possibility of having a child of their own) would soon change. It seems the prophet was there to give their most pressing desire a chance to be seen and, possibly, born.

A candlestick (lamp) in the room (calling awareness to what was missing in their rich home) was a reminder that a man of light (Lord Jesus Christ, in the person of Prophet Elisha) was in their home and could bring God's light down to them. Yahweh, our Lord Jesus, wants His children to experience joy and gladness.

One day, after many visits to his room on the wall (roof), the woman's desire was fulfilled. The man of God observed that he needed to express his gratitude to the woman and her husband for the gift of a place to rest his tired body. What was peculiar before then was that he hadn't noticed any little ones running around but had not asked why there weren't any, perhaps just as an oversight.

Prophet Elisha was more concerned about facilitating a social connection between her family and other influential people in their town of Shumen. He was quickly made aware by his servant, Gehazi (a divine connector, facilitator, and helper), that the family needed a son, and by God, she would have one and all would be well in their wealth (loving home) and riches (abundance of material resources).

Gifts of God may not have expiration dates on them. Otherwise, God would not give these gifts to us. God alone changes our times and seasons. Sarah (of Abraham) was ninety years old when God visited her and she had her son, Isaac.

God's righteous ones have many afflictions. The Lord delivers us from them. This kind woman had overcome barrenness. She had a son now by the power of our Master Holy Spirit. We come to know about this woman because of how God uniquely positioned her to be of help to the prophet of God and what ensued.

God is always seeking those who will showcase His glory. God can appear to be silent during these times, though He is looking for someone in need of His graces.

We are reminded that the earth is the Lord's, but there are conditions for ascending the mountain of the Lord: clean hands, a pure heart, trust in God, money in the well of families/individuals must be shared, and not swearing by other gods.

What do you do when the miracle dies? Something diabolical had happened to the Shunammite woman and her family. The miracle child, a son, was dead. He died suddenly in the arms of his mother from a bad headache. All seemed lost—a mockery of God of sorts by the Old Serpent.

"The thief, comes but to steal, kill, and to destroy," but our Lord Jesus Christ "came to give us believers the abundance of life in Him" (John 10:10b).

We recognize the supremacy of God over death and burial. We are not to give up in times of adversity, for our knowledge of the sovereignty of God over all situations must rise.

Our Master Holy Spirit shared with me that to disconnect from life may be the death of one, but burial (life without God in it) is the real death.

We know courage in the storm is what the Shunammite woman lovingly showed, following the sudden death of the miracle child, her only son. She stirred at death in her son, kept him connected to the living, and stopped the plans of the Old Serpent to move him progressively into burial. Let's examine the scriptures and see how our Master Holy Spirit says she did it.

We must at least have a mustard-seed faith. Our Lord Jesus requires it of us so we can see the majesty of God. It is a product of our connection to the power of resurrection, our Master Holy Spirit, our loving joining with Lord Jesus Christ in His death, burial, and resurrection.

The Shunammite woman rode on a donkey with her servant to look for the man of God—the only one she knew could help to bring back her dead child. The boy had been sick and suddenly had died. She left her home in haste, saying only "It is well" to all who asked her about the boy or her life, even her husband who had sent the servants to take the sick boy to her.

She had the winning strength to ride on a donkey, so she knew she could still reach God in the person of Prophet Elisha who had settled her in her home as a happy mother of a son, an heir. We are reminded that, somewhere in the future, our Lord Jesus Christ would ride on a donkey He had asked to be untied.

She looked into the future, saw the untying of a donkey and its colt by our Lord Jesus Christ—a setting free of sorts, of the prisoners of the Old Serpent—and believed her son too could be set free. Her loving son, a prisoner of the Old Serpent, now dead, needed to be released to accomplish his purpose on earth.

When we are called to stand for God, we must know the enemy will show up. In all things and happenings in our lives, we must still give thanks to God.

The Shunammite woman was in the spirit, reading in scriptures in search of our Lord Jesus Christ, God. Giving thanks activates God's grace. Lovingly, God had now given this woman the grace for a child of her own, but cunningly, the Old Serpent had come for him.

The boy had been taken to his mother, the one who had sought for him. We must stand with unwavering faith. Whatever was wrong with the boy was in his head. He sat on her lap, a place of rest, and there he died at noon (i.e., in the prime of life).

Believing in the awesomeness of God, in deep sorrow, this woman placed a demand on the everlasting one to honor Himself. Our Lord Jesus Christ reminded us that on earth we will encounter tribulations, but we are not to worry but to take heart, for He has overcome these problems.

The naked eye (loving and helpful people) would have seen the death of the boy as a lost cause. Right away, she shut out the naked eye. No naked eye saw the boy, and none considered her efforts a lost cause, giving hope to the situation. Off she went in search of the prophet with the knowledge of how to call God into stopping the burial of her only child.

Our Master Holy Spirit taught me, through the man of God Nana Bentil, that my placement of my right hand on my right lap during prayer was a request for God to quickly act on behalf of my son. This gesture, when praying for him, had been released to me several weeks earlier by our Master without an explanation as to its spiritual meaning and power.

Prophet Bentil said our Master told him to ask me to put my right hand on my right lap to bring his spirit into the moment as we were about to pray for my son.

I screamed in excitement, for looming in the future was an eerie situation that was about to come upon him. In the moments we are not able to do that, the mercy of God's loving still speaks for us. But now I was enlightened about a spiritual key for sons accessing heaven when parents' knees are on the ground for them.

Our Master Holy Spirit is likely to show other divine strategies to our parents for ushering our sons and daughters into His awesome presence, but this He gave to me in my time of great need. I understand more clearly now the mystery the Lord had been trying to get me to unearth, but the state of my spiritual antenna, which was clogged by life's occurrences, had prevented its blessed understanding.

However, speaking to the man of God on this wonderful day and asking for backup prayers, I keyed into this revelation, and it would become a major prayer posture for me when in need of a divine blessing for him, which is always. Therefore, I have some understanding of what positioning a sick or dying boy on his mother's lap may mean. It may bring God's glory and saving graces down into the situation. Lovingly, the Shunammite woman knew that God's eye had already descended upon the boy. God's power and authority over death, and burial, would soon be laid bare for all to see. The son was strategically positioned now to receive life from God, opposing the purpose of the Old Serpent over his life. You can hear his mother's voice saying to God, "What profit is there in my blood, when I go down to the pit? Shall the dust praise thee? Shall it declare thy truth? Hear, O Lord, and have mercy upon me: Lord, be thou my helper" (Psalm 30:9–10).

When a person's head is hurt, the entire body follows. We lovingly find on the boy's head many wonderful elements of life. God, in the person of Prophet Elijah, must now take it back positionally:

- hair: the glory of God on the head (The boy lovingly carried this glory on him.)
- skull: God's covering using earth over mankind's head, the covering of humans to counter the surrounding of earth
- eye: God's blessing of a mirror to the soul, mankind's courageous vision into the spirit, mankind gaining insights to reign honorably
- ear: an instrument for hearing God's loving and instructive voice, a winning eavesdropping mechanism for gaining ground and monitoring the Old Serpent's actions

- nose: the Master Holy Spirit's breath (passage) in mankind and His mindfulness, mankind's glorious breath to subdue the Old Serpent in their lives
- mouth: the loving voice of God's glorious praise of mankind, the voice of desperate, grieving, loving, and honoring of God and mankind
- chin: the cast of major protection of God over mankind's wonderful mouth gate, mind-boggling power and authority of mankind over the courageous weapons of the Old Serpent
- jawbone: the gracious wire God lovingly gives mankind, as power over situations brought by the Old Serpent
- teeth: God's weapon against people of the world, foes, and the Old Serpent, gladness and blessings given to mankind
- neck: strength and power God gives to prevent burdens from yoking mankind's ability to influence the heads of others, major wisdom that moves mankind into a place of wealth, productivity, and achievements in life

It goes, then, that the minding of one's head is vital to the body, for the grace for living is controlled by one's head. If a person's head is wounded, it affects his mindfulness and his ability to achieve purpose.

The Shunammite woman's son's head was dead, so she went looking for the one who had the power to bring heaven down to settle her case: Prophet Elisha. She left riding on a donkey, knowing that work done for the Lord speaks for the servants of God.

These parents' lives were shutting down again, challenging the authority of God who had given them love, joy, gladness, favor, and riches with the birth of their little boy. The Shunammite woman laid the body of her dead son on Prophet Elisha's bed. Before the Lord she laid the lifeless body of her beloved son. Heaven was in close contact with the prophet; she now had to find him.

The room being on the wall (roof) meant the prophet would be praying for them with clarity of mind (as if putting on the helmet of salvation), having an excellent clairvoyance and a gracious spirit.

The Shunammite woman asked her servant to saddle her donkey (mingling wealth and grief), and off they went in search of Prophet Elisha. Prophet Elisha was at Mount Carmel, the same place where earlier Prophet Elijah had laid a challenge to Jezebel's four hundred or so false prophets of Baal and won.

When the Shunammite woman reached Elisha, the prophet, she took hold of his feet. It was the feet, the Gospel of truth, that had brought him into their lives making her a mother when the Old Serpent had made her barren. His feet carried good news, and she would be needing that again. But God had not revealed the incident to the prophet, for God alone chooses when to speak.

She said to Prophet Elisha, "Did I desire a son of my lord? Did I not say, 'Do not deceive me?'" (2 Kings 4:28). Prophet Elisha followed her home to see the boy who was dead but who was not yet buried. He was invested in this case, and God must act now. His servant Gehazi was sent ahead with specific instructions on how to raise the boy.

He went ahead as instructed but couldn't accomplish the task, because the opening of gates, which was required in this situation, must involve heaven already awaiting a request from a prophet. Gehazi, his servant, was sent, but the gates needed an authoritative and powerful man of God's voice. God, the Father, God, the Son, and God, the Holy Ghost, in agreement with Prophet Elisha, will provide the grace for life.

The boy's head was attacked. The Old Serpent thought the gift was already dead and buried. But would God allow this son of man to pass to burial, to eternity?

God told the Old Serpent that the seed of a woman (the carrier of divine love) would bruise his head. The Old Serpent would try to attack the head of this son, thinking this was the Promised Seed who would bruise his head.

The Old Serpent had clearly missed the destructive and diabolical assignment he had reserved for the Son of Man, our Lord Jesus Christ.

The boy was but a foreshadowing of the coming birth, death, and burial of our Lord Jesus Christ. Prophet Elisha, standing in place of our Lord Jesus Christ, to release the boy, commanded the gates of unbelief, death, and burial—immortality—to lift up their heads. Our Master Holy Spirit said evil rose to question Prophet Elisha. Among other things, he asked the unmoved prophet whether the woman was morally and socially righteous.

This tells us that what we give to God is given back to us more than a seven fold. The prophet would restore the life of this vessel to showcase God's goodness and power.

We want to see how this was done, because this woman stands to encourage us about trusting in God, giving God our best, and standing strong in the face of unimaginable pain because we know the God we serve.

The Shunammite woman had boldly provided food and shelter for the prophet of God, winning a moral victory through obedience. Caring for the prophet also earned her a prophet's reward, an heir, fulfilling her social obligations. They were now morally and socially righteous.

Prophet Elisha moved to open the gates to release the woman's miracle son. He went in and shut the door on the two of them (logically and spiritually). The man of God was praying, leaving earth for heaven in the spirit so death, which had come over him, would release him.

The miracle of the birth of a son had yet to satisfy the Shunammite woman that God was the loving giver of life. But if God would raise her boy from death and burial and open the gates of joy and gladness, it would make it all real to her.

Prophet Elisha paced back and forth in his room at the top—"heaven." With the light of God shining through him, he devised a supernatural method for raising the son of this good woman and her husband from death.

The prophet lovingly stretched his ammunition (his body, spirit, and soul) over the boy who was dead but not yet buried. The prophet's ammunition was cooperatively and divinely aligned with the boy's spirit, soul, and body, though he was moving fast toward burial. He did it this way:

- mouth to mouth (stillness of death to the speech of life—the boy is to live, with the power to prophesy)
- eye to eye (light of life—the knowledge to pull down graven images in the family and to see clearly, as beholding a divine mirror showing divine images in the future)
- hand to hand (gracious blessings of spiritual upliftment in the boy, to loosen the lives of others, not to be upended by premature death)
- leg to leg (moving progressively into a newer and more wonderful dimension of knowledge of God, moving from death to life in the physical realm and in the spiritual)

The power of life and death are in the power of the tongue of Prophet Elisha who aligned (mouth to mouth) his mouth with the boy's to verbally command the gates of burial before them to lift their heads.

Prophet Elisha waited for light from God to flow into the boy through his eyes (eye to eye), and the two moved gradually toward life with God in it, life of light. Two more hurdles remained.

Prophet Elisha aligned (hand to hand) his hands and the boy's in true worship of God. The prophet's hands over the boy's (wonderfully laid), and divinely guided, he prayed.

The boy was the heir to his father's riches of earthly worship. If restored to life, the family would build a monument of true worship of God (sustaining the flow of true wealth in God).

We are privileged to be worshippers of Lord Jesus Christ. This family was about to learn just that, moving from being regular worshippers to worshippers of God in spirit and in truth. Lonely and moving toward his burial, the boy needed Prophet Elisha to change his direction in life.

Prophet Elisha had to align (leg to leg) his legs and the boy's legs, asking the gates of death and burial to release the boy's legs. These legs would walk where God would send him in the future to release the captives of Israel.

Lord Jesus Christ was coming to change humanity's eternal death to one of eternal life with Him. The ground in which He would be buried would have no power over Him. He faced burial (eternal life without God) brought about by the sins of mortal man, Adam, but would rise again from the dead to bring mankind back into eternal life with God, by Himself, the Old Serpent notwithstanding.

The posture Prophet Elisha took in the fight to bring back the dead boy from burial is known as "divine elongation."

The Master Holy Spirit gave the word and this explanation on divine elongation. Let's now follow along . . .

> El = God, the Creator of the heavens and the earth
>
> on = pained, and in agony, stretched out Himself wonderfully to free mankind
>
> ga = wounded for mankind, I understand your limitation(s), Prophet Elisha
>
> tion = the stretched one, the prophet, moving divinely in the spirit to end the burial of the good son

Prophet Elisha stretched himself fully over the dead boy in a glorious adoration of God, got the boy's body warmed, and prepared him to receive back the life that had left him. The Bible tells us that Prophet Elisha then turned away and walked back and forth in the room. This was a movement to pageant the power and authority of the soon-coming king, Lord Jesus Christ, over death and burial, making a public show of the Devil. The prophet was aware of our Lord Jesus Christ. He had searched the scriptures. The prophet stretched himself over the body, a gesture of calling upon our Master Holy Ghost to stop the boy's progress to burial.

After his prophetic actions, the boy sneezed seven times, moving him back to life. The breath of God Almighty now in him, the boy opened his eyes. Prophet Elisha had completed the wonderfully laid plan of God to recover the boy from the hands of the Old Serpent, restored him back to life, and place in the hands of his anxious parents. "Make a joyful noise unto the LORD, all ye lands" (Psalm 100:1).

The Master Holy Spirit says the opening of closed gates is unusual. The boy, by sneezing seven times, unusually changed the order of death and burial. Our God sneezed to move the boy back to life.

Issues concerning the Shunammite woman appears again in 2 Kings 8. Prophet Elisha once again intervened to ensure she received back what belonged to her, having left her home country for another land because of famine. Scripture lets us know that, when she returned home after seven years (ceasing to stay in the lying Old Serpent's territory) in Philistia, the Shunammite woman discovered her properties had been taken over by those who stayed behind.

The Shunammite woman appealed to (went before God) King Jehoram (whose name means "Jehovah is exalted" (https://en.wikipedia.org/wiki/Jehoram#:~:text=Jehoram), and God exalted

Himself. Once again with help from Prophet Elisha, they recovered all their lost possessions. However, the prophet's connection with influential people in Shumen was essential and useful this time around. By these connections, she recovered all her lost properties.

Our Master Holy Spirit let us know that women are always fighting for the survival of mankind. He said it was because of her that, once more, God restored the wealth that had been taken from this loving family. Our Lord Jesus Christ would come to fish for men, and women would be an important part of His looming earthly journey.

The Rabbinical tradition holds the Shunammite woman's son to have been our very own Prophet Habakkuk, one of several minor prophets in the Bible. Believers would have missed this wonderful prophet but for the anointed woman of God's fight for her son.

The Shunammite woman's story points us to a life of victory over evil in the present, as well as in the future, when our Lord Jesus Christ will come again, greatly to be praised. In the meantime, we should live in ways that make our lives shout-outs to God, our creator and sustainer. Anything is possible when we work lovingly with God, even in the face of insurmountable odds.

CHAPTER 9

Conclusion: The Master Holy Spirit

The women examined in this book may not look like the women we see today or have in our lives. These women from our Bible stories seem to have been anointed and well put together. We suffer from the same qualified fate they experienced in times past. But they were the blessed of God, and they could not have completed their role assignments without the help of our Master Holy Spirit. Only with His help was I able to write this book.

Before our Lord Jesus Christ's ascension to heaven, He told His disciples He would not leave them orphaned but would send another comforter who would bring to their remembrance everything He had taught them during His earthly ministry. Lord Jesus Christ gave us the Holy Spirit to teach us, mentor us, and guide us in our faith walks on earth, and He is our healer. He is our helper, advocate, revealer of truths and mysteries, giver of all spiritual gifts, and much more.

Our very patient Master Holy Spirit sat with me to unpack the mysteries found in this book, shedding new light on the roles of seven godly women who participated in God's loving work to return mankind to Him, even to our Lord Jesus Christ. There are also anecdotes about today's women, whose works and good concerns made their inclusion relevant.

The Master Holy Spirit is known as the wind of God, river of life, finger of God, breath of God, strength of God, power of God, pillar of cloud, pillar of fire, and much more. He is called our mind regulator, joy giver, counselor, silencer of our foes, the one who puts evil under our feet, the spirit and inspiration of the Word of God, ensuring wisdom, flame of fire, and thongs of fire. During the writing of this book, and the selection of the women included here, I gladly experienced many of these attributes of the Master.

I hope those who read this book would have experiences of their own to tell of, drawing from the guardian Spirit who orchestrated its good writing.

Know that our Master Holy Spirit is the compassionate understanding, laughter, and support we offer those in need; the loving-kindness we show our kin, friends, bosses, peers, and colleagues; the hungry we help feed; the elderly we bless with our time, love, money, care, and love; and much more.

As you read this book, may you find in your own life's journey the strength and wisdom of the women whose lives and roles are examined here unabashedly.

In writing this book, I came to understand and appreciate our Master Holy Spirit and the importance of His presence in our lives.

He can help change the directions of things in our lives, eliminate our sorrows, and dry up the floods that surround us and our families because of the winning relationships we have with God. Let's seek to know Him more.

We know that, like the women in this book, we can rise gloriously to fulfill mind-bending assignments. Our generation of women are expected to win souls for our Lord Jesus Christ, raise godly children who will do exploits, obey parents so their days may be longer and blessed, and easily, lovingly choose God over our traditions. May we receive the grace to crush evil where and when it gives off a scent of humming disobedience and move in timely fashion with God-given plans.

There may never be other "greats" of the Lord such as those examined here: Holy Mary, Eve, Rahab, Hannah, Ruth, Queen Esther, and the Shunammite Woman. Yet God has lovingly given honor to women with great wisdom and strength in the persons of our grandmothers, mothers, aunts, daughters, sisters, nieces, cousins, friends, ministers, bosses, women leaders who will take on various courageous roles, and other ammunitions (spirits, souls, and bodies) to lead generations of women, including the lost and the sick.

This book is a good example of the work
of our Master Holy Spirit.